NakedHR-the 7 Deadly Sins That Make HR Departments Suck

Trent Cotton

First Printing: 2018

ISBN: 978-0-359-14732-8

TABLE OF CONTENTS

INTRODUCTION

Let's Get Naked

There once was a place of paradise. All of the plants bore fruit, the waters in the rivers and streams were clean and alive with fish. As you walked through this paradise, the vibrancy of life was all around you. You could hear all of the sounds of the multitudes of animals dancing through a green carpeted landscape of ecstatic joy. It was nothing less than perfect.

There was a man and woman who lived there. They were free to roam through paradise with little concern for the usual troubles of life. Their nakedness was not known to them because everything in their world was perfect.

Balance.

Anxiety did not exist. No judgment. All of this in a perfect world thought only to be in fairy tales and all while completely naked.

Along comes a snake, an evil character who convinces them to break the only law in this paradise. They were forbidden to eat from the Tree of Wisdom for if they did, they would know all. When they violated this sacred law, everything changed.

If you read the story of Eden from the Book of Genesis in the Bible, what was the first thing Adam and Eve realized when they were "enlightened"? They realized they were naked. Before paradise was ruined, the two of them walked shamelessly throughout paradise without ever realizing they were naked. Now, they felt shame and wanted to cover the magnificent creation they were formed to be.

I fear all of us suffer from a form of this. Whether you believe in the Christian Bible or not, you have to admit that it is interesting the comparison of how life was before and after they gained "enlightenment" and became aware of their nakedness. Some thousands of years later, as professionals, we suit up to hide our nakedness. We hide our fears, our shortcomings, our anxiety... ultimately hiding our humanity behind layers of dark clothing.

If there is one group of professionals I have encountered who love to cover themselves in guises of policies, procedures, risk mitigation, and anything else that sounds like it could be a barrier to a successful business, it's most Human Resources departments.

I was early in my career in banking and only one week into my first management role when I first interacted with an HR professional. There was an employee in my branch who was not meeting their numbers, spoiling the morale for my new team and they needed to go. I calmly presented my case with all of the evidence I thought I needed to get HR's blessing to terminate this cancerous plague in my office.

Well, I soon learned how wrong I was.

Over the next year, I formed a contentious relationship with the HR group at the bank and even earned what I called my "designated chair of punishment" in the HR wing at the corporate tower. I was young in my career so there were things I had to prove to myself and my colleagues but I felt like my most significant obstacle was the great Wizard of Oz in the Ivory Tower of Doom.

One of my least proud moments was when I lost my temper with an employee playing the system, leveraging her "lawyer on retainer" (though I never thought she had one) and the FMLA leave policy. She would call in sick or take a leave and then members of my team would see her out gallivanting around town later, perfectly fine and seems to have the time of her life. I felt as if she was making a fool of me in front of my team and HR was letting her get away with it.

So, in one of my unprofessional moves, I confronted her in front of the team to show my Alpha status in the office. When she retorted back something smart ass, I blew sideways and used numerous conjugations of superlatives that made me feel better but also made me look like a fool.

I remember telling my assistant manager that when HR called, tell them I was already on my way.

Fast forward ten years and I find myself working as a contract recruiter for another financial institution. My first six months was to train with three "HR Professionals" who seemed to make it a point to tell me daily, if not at least weekly, that I would never make it in the industry because I didn't know HR. They would give me the shit jobs they didn't want to work on because they did not like the manager or the roles were just not deemed as sexy enough for someone at their level.

At the beginning of the contract period, I felt very insecure about my potential for success. This was a new feeling for me and it affected me to the core of who I thought I was. I started to believe the "HR Professionals" who said I'd never make it and that they had bets on when I would quit.

Things changed with one meeting.

Ralph, one of the executives I was working with, began a meeting with me by ranting about how much he hated HR. They were slow, didn't know his business, always said no, never took time to take risks, etc. At the end of his little temper tantrum, I shocked him when I said, "You know, I completely agree!"

I went on to say, "I wonder sometimes what the hell I'm doing in this group. I hate HR too!"

Believe it or not, that started a series of conversations that helped me find my own voice in a profession I thought I was not cut out for. Ralph introduced me to his fellow executives and direct reports as "the guy I was telling you about in HR." The next couple of months included invites with Ralph and the team to go have dinner and drinks as well as invites to their strategy meetings where I had free reign to ask direct, business-related questions.

After working as a contractor for one year for this financial firm, I began forming closer relationships with my internal clients than I had with my HR team members. I can't say that helped my standing on the team, but it did catch the eye of the HR Executive we all reported to. She asked to come with me to one of my client meetings and observe. I knew this was a step in the process she took to evaluate whether to hire someone full time.

So there I was, sitting with my clients, laughing about one of the previous week's drinking sessions when I remembered: Oh shit, my boss's boss is in this meeting. It was an internal WTF moment for sure. So I took a risk and remembered that my client liked me for who I was and what I brought to the table. They would often make comments like, "I forget you're in HR sometimes."

I took a deep breath. I centered myself. Then I engaged in the meeting as if my observer were not in the room.

During that meeting, Ralph and his team were discussing some business changes they felt needed to be made which included hiring additional staff to accomplish the goal. When I was asked for my opinion, I silenced the room with one question: What the hell are you thinking?

My client group got a laugh but I noticed my observer never cracked a smile. Actually, she had the same stone face she had when she sat down. I thought to myself, "Great, well I just fucked the opportunity for me to go full time!"

Throughout the rest of the meeting, I followed up my question to the team by explaining that I had looked at some of the production of their current staff and determined it made more sense to eliminate the unproductive, lower 25% and wait six months before hiring anyone else. I challenged them to take a risk and see if we didn't see an increase in revenue and profit before just adding more losers to a drowning ship.

They took the risk. I will confess I was only half right. Profits did go up, but not as much as I told my clients they would. Nonetheless, I felt like I had arrived. This was who I was to be in the HR industry, even if it was not with the firm I was currently working for.

On the elevator ride down, my HR executive asked if we could go grab lunch. I remember thinking that this was going to be the lunch where she let me go. The anxious pit of acid in my stomach grew with every passing floor despite my best attempts to remain positive.

During lunch, there were a couple of moments of small talk about family or the weather. The seeming delay of the inevitable was killing me. After several periods of awkward silence, I decided to bite the bullet and ask my HR Executive how she thought I performed in the meeting.

"I loved it."

Hold the damn press...what did she just say? She loved it? Am I being punked? Is someone going to run out to the table with cameras and say, got ya?

"I think you're exactly what I want on my team. You don't hold back, there's no politics with you and more importantly, you know your business. You were talking about shit in there I didn't even understand, but your client did and that's all that matters."

That was a career-defining moment. I took the risk, determined who I wanted to be and said the hell with the consequences.

As I write this introduction, I have been in HR for close to 15 years. My reputation for understanding my client's business, not having the best choice of words and a point-blank approach to HR has given me some pretty unique opportunities. Actually, the best part has been the deep and long-lasting relationships I have formed with my clients over the years.

In this book, I want to "Get Naked" with you. No, not that way, but I do want to strip down what we do as HR professionals. I want to challenge you to remember why you actually got into the industry-THE PEOPLE. I feel too many HR departments forget the HUMAN aspect of the role and place more importance on processes than people. Unfortunately, decades of this approach to managing the HUMAN aspect of a company has tarnished the HR reputation and has also allowed too many mediocre professionals into our ranks.

I have surveyed my network and several social media channels to ask why people hate working with HR. The responses have been somewhat predictable but still worth exploring. With this information, I have created a list of "Deadly Sins of HR" for you to avoid.

The Deadly Sins have come from my interactions with company leaders, feedback from polls on LinkedIn and life experiences. If you are looking for an HR self-help book packed full of stories that will be soup for your soul... Sorry, wrong book. This will be an in your face, raw, and unfiltered challenge to UP your game.

The title of the book is NAKEDHR, do you really think I plan to dress anything up for you?

So, with that, LET'S GET NAKED!

STAY CONNECTED!

- Subscribe to my <u>YouTube Channel: NakedHR</u>

- Visit my Blog at <u>NAKEDHR.ME</u> and join the conversation

CHAPTER 1

Be Like Wendy Rhoades and KNOW your Business

HR Deadly Sin: They don't know my business, only HR.

On the Showtime hit series "Billions", Maggie Siff plays Wendy Rhoades, an in-house performance coach and all around badass for Axe Capital. Although the character is a trained psychiatrist, she uses her keen understanding of the human psyche and knowledge of the company's inner workings and profit targets as a way to position to be invaluable to the company, its employees and most importantly, the founder and CEO. She is a power player in the supercharged and ultra-competitive world of finance and a woman who should never be underestimated. Her job is to motivate and coach the firm's employees to exceed beyond what they feel they can do. In case you have not seen the show, do not get this image of a loving, nurturing character who uses psychiatric training to help make everyone get along in the office. *No!* Wendy is a brash, direct and ultimate warrior. That is why I think she is a perfect example of how a NakedHR professional should be.

Why?

She does not hide behind a kindergarten teacher personality to try to make sure everyone is in line with the corporate initiatives. Wendy is typically an "in your face, say what's on your mind" consultant and has a deep understanding of how the business works. Her knowledge of the business helps her know what levers need to be pulled to achieve success and how to leverage the company's talent to achieve their goals. She addresses issues when they happen, head on and never pulls any punches. Her tenacity, intellect and interpersonal relationships help her to become the in-house confidant, coach, and HR director.

Honestly, that's what a successful NakedHR professional look like in my opinion. How do you do it? It's easier than you think. The goal for the NakedHR professional is to get out from behind the glass or wooden doors of your safe place and venture into the jungle where your client is. There is a land of opportunity for both of you to be uncomfortable and grow together toward success.

When you entrench yourself in the business, your partners will begin to come to you for more than just HR. They'll begin bouncing any idea or issue related to the talent on their team which is what you want. More importantly, if you are that involved in the business, you will find yourself seeking out the executives you support with ideas, feedback, or updates on a more impromptu basis. This type of exchange will allow you to position yourself as the "invaluable" member of the executive team and not the wizard in the tower.

According to the Harvard Business Review's post in July of 2015, one of traditional HR's toughest obstacles is supporting business strategy because it's always a moving target. In comparison to the short-term planning needed in business strategies, HR is a long-term play. The article asserts HR can better align itself to the business strategy while making itself invaluable by analyzing the short-term needs against the projects HR deems important. Rather than being reactive to business needs, the astute NakedHR professional will deal with the immediate issue while also taking some time to better understand the implications on the business long term. Additionally, the NakedHR professional should spend time analyzing market conditions to determine any trends that should be addressed in the immediate or foreseeable future.

To be successful, begin with an in-depth analysis of the company or department you are assigned to support. Use industry knowledge paired with hands-on research to provide the ultimate value to the firms you support. Encourage the executives to open the kimono! This has always been a requirement when I took on a new client or department but I'd like to be positive and say the other part was because I made the atmosphere inviting enough for them to be comfortable enough to do it. As we go over the steps to become more involved with the client, remember that this will be a slow process. Adoption of the business to willingly invite their HR partner to meetings, planning sessions and outings can be longer in organizations where the HR department functioned more like a hall monitor than a helpful friend. Here are some stages I have seen in this process.

Stage 1: Settle for Small Steps

The process of becoming included can be as simple as asking your client if you can attend their planning meetings. Perhaps you should start with smaller steps and agree to meet with the manager for lunch or coffee every other week, just to start a routine. Start small and work your way into the meetings with their team.

One of my favorite mentors was a Senior Lender for a bank I worked at while in college. He was in his sixties and I in my twenties but I'd like to think we made a good team. He was an incredibly wise and patient man whose clients adored him. After going on a few meetings with him, I began to learn why.

"Mr. Joe", as he was called by clients and coworkers alike, was always jovial. Even in client meetings, he would cut jokes with the staff and the owners. He always had this curiosity about him and would constantly ask questions about the business's products and the processes they used to produce them.

One day, I asked Mr. Joe why he always asked questions about the business and never really sold anything. Boy did he school me!

I learned that day his questions to better understand the business was his secret weapon to understanding what products the client needed. His approach was always to provide products to not only meet a need but also deepen a client relationship. I cannot tell you how many times I have used that little piece of knowledge while meeting with clients and prospect. Ask questions, learn all you can about your client. That is the first step in becoming invaluable.

Stage 2: Develop Trust & Start with Lunch

Like I referenced above, an easy and less invasive step is to begin having lunch with key leaders and employees within the organization you support. One of the benefits of doing every other week coffee or lunch is ability for the HR partner to steer away from HR topics. I mean, who really wants to talk about HR stuff over lunch right? Ironically, as you keep the small talk as your main goal, you'll find the client opening up about other items in their office. That's when you know you're breaking down those walls.

In this stage, try to "get naked" with the manager by sharing some of your story. Be real with them and let them know they can be real with you. I have found sharing a little of my personal life helps the other person know it's ok to share with me. As I have mentioned before, sometimes these moments are the most important because it helps us get a better understanding of our client. Like Wendy Rhoades, we sometimes have to use a little psychology to understand why people do what they do before we can find a solution to some of the issues we need to tackle. Our job is to be a coach, manager and counselor which can seem overwhelming but rarely do I feel overwhelmed when having a deeper conversation with my client over lunch. It typically reminds me that the reason I love HR is the human element. Once I am reminded of this, being a coach, manager and counselor is second nature because it's all about the human I'm sitting across from at the time.

Stage 3: Random Loveliness

Ok, I know that sounds weird but it really says a lot about the developing relationship you are working on when the manager calls you for something random to get your insight. There have been times when I have worked with consultants or had a consultant who worked for me who complained about the "random" question their client called with. After I spent a minute throat punching that consultant in my head, I would explain to them this is where the gold is in the relationship building process.

Think about it from your client's point of view.

* "Should I call them and ask them that? It's not related to HR?"

* After some time thinking: "No I'll look stupid. Maybe I could ask... no, they won't know."

* Later in the day, "Oh what the hell, if they don't know maybe they can point me to someone who does."

The risk taken by the client is looking dumb. I have met very few managers who enjoy looking dumb so that is why I see this little peak of a hope as gold. In that one step, the manager told you two things:

1. They feel they can be vulnerable with you and
2. They're giving you a test to see if you'll actually come through.

14

I once had a client who ran a manufacturing plant that produced some items for the construction agency. They were a brutal bunch of leaders but I kind of liked it. It was hard for them to see me more as the consultant to "keep them out of trouble" and it took me a while to develop any type of relationship outside of the contract.

One day, I was onsite and one of the senior executives asked permission, "Can I ask you a random question?"

"Sure" I responded, silently praying he was not going to ask me anything about the manufacturing process because I was still learning.

"Why do you think our numbers aren't improving? I mean business is booming but our profit is still the same. Why do you think that is the case?"

So in my own true style I first asked permission to speak freely. Once granted, I began asking a series of questions to better understand what some of the causes could be. Since this was not an HR question, I asked more pointed questions about the business model, processes and finances. Some of the questions included:

- What's your cash flow look like? Are you using credit to fund the cycle between production and sale or do you have other arrangements?
- Has the price of the materials increased or is there something going on in the market causing this?

- Are you selling only on price?
- What's the percentage you pay your salespeople on closed business?

Before long, both of us realized we had been chatting for an hour about solutions and had some really good ones that we wanted to beta test. That's when I knew I had finally begun chipping away at the company. That afternoon opened a series of dialogues where we worked as a team to make the company more efficient and profitable. If I had discounted his questions as not pertaining to HR, I could have lost out on a great working relationship with the client as well as some pretty fun outings we had during our working relationship. I remember the executive even joked later that he didn't realize "I could do business stuff too".

Using our example of Wendy Rhoades, she is a pro at this step. On the show, she'll have employees stop in to ask random questions about their business or some childhood memory that's affecting their performance. Her stature in the company is one of trusted advisor with no subject specificity. Think about your clients, do they only ask you HR related questions or do you two get into the weeds of their business, the market or changes in product lines? If not, you're missing a great opportunity to develop yourself and alleviate some of the monotony that is associated with any job. Don't miss out on this opportunity to deepen the relationships with your clients by learning more about what they do.

Stage 4: Monkey see monkey do

I know a number of professionals who make it all the way through stage 3 and then bomb stage 4 which is the easiest. Rather than showing up in attire to match their client, they go for the stuffy business suit or a lighter version of it. What's worse is that the HR person comes in speaking that corporate bullshit language like a high school cheerleader who only knows how to speak cheer.

NO, NO. NO. Please, No!

If your goal is to get naked with your client, leave all of that BS at your emerald tower. If not, then you have wasted time working to develop the relationship. Let me explain.

I was working with a client in a very professional field where they enjoyed, or at least seemed to enjoy, suiting up every day. They would promenade around the office in their "latest" tailored suit or sport coat just like a peacock strutting to find a mate. Women would tout their own tailored wear but it was usually the purse and shoe game that they played the most. Although I love a good suit and have a number of them in the closet, it just isn't me. I like being in jeans and a t-shirt most of the time because it's one less decision I have to make. The game of what suit goes with what shirt which matches what tie... oh do I want to wear colorful socks or keep it conservative? Ugh, just writing all of that exhausts me.

But one thing I noticed about this office during some observations was the lack of genuine concern for each other.

Everyone was so busy suiting up to impress their peers that no one seemed to know anything about their coworkers outside of what they wore. I promise I am not exaggerating.

So when I showed up to a management team offsite wearing jeans and a V-neck t-shirt, high tops, and a light jacket, you can nearly imagine the looks I got. It was as if someone farted in church when I walked in. All of them stared at me as I spoke to some of the senior managers. Honestly, I felt kind of naked with all of them staring the way they were.

As I led one of the opening exercises with the team, I finally just had enough. This buttoned up crew had finally reached that nerve. The nerve that usually causes me to speak a little more freely. The one that enables me to find the jugular in any situation and just go for it. Sometimes it's messy but other times its pretty damn needed. Both happened in this situation.

So while mid-sentence, I finally stopped and asked, "Can someone tell me what the hell is making everyone stare at what I'm wearing? Is my ass hanging out of it or something?"

There were a few chuckles but I just said the only two curse words I had ever heard said in that organization. (Yeah, they were a little boring.)

So one of the more tenured leaders felt the need to get up to explain that their culture did not endorse the wearing of jeans to corporate function. There was nothing wrong with what she said but more in how she said it. It was almost as if she looked down her nose at me while scolding me like the nuns used to in school.

"So are you done?" I asked. Again, silent gasps.

"We are here to talk about how this room of managers and leaders can empower, motivate and engage your employees and all you seem to be worried about is that I wore jeans to a corporate function? You pay me to produce, not put on a show."

I felt like I just threw a baseball in my neighbor's window. You know, that silence you have right as you watch the ball move uncontrollably toward that window as if in slow motion? Yeah, that's what was going on in the room at that very moment.

That was the turning point in the exercise. It was the breaking of glass that allowed some of the managers to finally open up to their peers. Most shared how they felt confined and restricted, unable to empower their teams because they were not empowered. This began several conversations among the team members about how to change their culture from control to empower and engage. All they needed was a little push.

If I had gone into that meeting and acted like the corporate HR consultant pushover, I would have committed malpractice. My job in that meeting was to break their mold. Not necessarily get them to start wearing jeans but at least start opening their mind to new ways of working. Their competition was eating their lunch because the company's attention to rule following meant their attention to innovation and growing with the times was nonexistent.

Over time, I started to notice some of the managers would go without a tie or a high class blouse. On Fridays, some of them

19

would start wearing khakis and a polo or boat shoes with an outfit and encourage their teams to do the same. Before long, the morale in the office changed, not because of the attire but because of the mindset.

Sometimes you have to set the tone and break out of what HR has always been and evolve to the HR your client needs. If they dress down, you dress down. If they use colorful language, you try the same or at least allow them to without judgement. It's quite easy and more importantly, pretty damn fun.

When you have arrived:

It was late one afternoon and I found myself sitting on a call with my Director and one of the executives my team and I supported. As usual, the conversation pertained to the perception the executive had about the level of support they were receiving from my team. Preceding the call, I spoke with Chad, my team member who supported this division, to get the low down.

Chad is a young guy with roughly three years of recruiting experience. He's a scrappy guy who's eager and extremely willing to receive coaching. In our debrief, he outlined for me what he had been doing to support this division as if he were giving a defense testimony. I knew Chad had a tendency to be unorganized but not providing service to his clients was not in his psyche.

So after the call with the executive, we agreed to set another call in two weeks to discuss progress. I provided some minor feedback to Chad about areas he could improve on based on both sides of the story. He agreed to work harder to "dazzle" this client to turn the perception.

One of the things I loved about Chad was his tenacity for knowing everything he could about the client and the role they were filling. He would usually go so far as to sit in on their product meetings and stand ups but not to provide updates on the search. His goal was to understand the product or service the teams were designing and/or building. These are the actions that helped him receive the praise from the executive while finding the candidates who blew away the hiring managers.

Only forty-five days later, Chad sent me a screenshot of a chat conversation he had with this executive regarding some of the candidates they had in the works. One line said it all,

"Chad, you are an invaluable member of my team."

Did you get that? She didn't say a valuable member of HR. Instead, she said Chad was an invaluable member of HER team. Chad had arrived!

It isn't a complicated process.

Sometimes HR needs to step out of the tower and get into the battle with their clients. Just like Chad, take some time to sit in on meetings for no other reason but to learn and listen. If you take this approach, you will learn more about the team and the needs they have. It won't be long before you position yourself like Wendy Rhoades: the in-house coach, HR subject matter expert, counselor and all around badass.

CHAPTER 2

Never Place Policies and Processes over People

Deadly Sin: HR values their policies and processes over the people it's supposed to be advocating for.

One of my favorite office related movies is Office Space. Although released in 1999, the humor regarding some of the stupid things we do in offices in name of productivity still apply.

In the movie, Ron Livingston finds himself in an unfulfilling, soul-sucking job he hates. He seeks help in the form of hypnotherapy to deal with the dreadful routines he has to live through daily. During one session, his hypnotherapist dies in the middle of the session, leaving him a constant state of not really giving a shit about much anything, including the crazy requirements placed on him in his job.

Before this unplanned alteration to his personality, Ron had to endure one of his managers who was the bane of his existence.

We all know these types. The corporate BS spewing, unproductive "manager" who delights in processes and reports while hiding behind the guise of caring for their team. His favorite question to ask is, "What about your TPS reports." The humor in the movie speaks to the complete disdain most of us feel about the corporate idolatry of processes and the loss of humanity in the workplace.

When I watch the movie now, I think of the numerous HR professionals I have worked with as a consultant or a colleague who treasured processes and prided themselves on being a stickler for following the code. They would rather have someone who is experiencing a life emergency fill out the right paperwork in the right color ink and faxed to the right number than simply doing what needs to be done to make someone feel valuable. Rather than talking about the effectiveness of continuous coaching and feedback, they would rather talk about how fancy their ten-page quarterly employee assessment process is. Instead of being engaged, goal-oriented humans, they are more like the automated phone lines that answer when you call into major organizations.

Sometimes, all we want to feel is valued, so why would ANYONE in Human Resources enjoy taking the human aspect out of it?

This was one of the questions I was asked by a manager in response to a questionnaire I sent to gather research on a company prior to working with them as a consultant. It seemed to resonate with every focus group of employees who felt like HR viewed them as nothing more than a number. One employee went so far as to say they felt more like an inmate than a valued employee.

Forbes.com released an article in July of 2016 entitled, "10 Reasons Everybody Hates HR". In its laundry list of offenses, two speak to the topic of processes and policies over people. They are:

- HR people talk more about policies, benefits and other announcements than they talk about culture, fear, trust, conflict or any of the million human issues that arise in every organization.
- HR people often have trouble seeing the "human side" of any issue, from a time-off request to a variation in a pay-grade or a hiring issue, focusing instead on keeping every process uniform and exception-free.

Think about your HR processes. Do they value the employee or do they only work to satisfy our need to CYA (cover your ass)? Don't misunderstand me, I value the process of documenting things but I do not value it over the employee. NakedHR professionals will get the job done to ensure the employee is taken care of and then handle the needed processes on the backend. Our job is to remove roadblocks, whether it be people or processes, to allow the company to achieve its goals. Unfortunately, many leaders in organizations feel HR is the roadblock from accomplishing their goals. Why?

A US based survey of 500 managers found a majority of them (36%) spend up to half of their day handling administrative tasks. The NakedHR professional is a roadblock blaster. We are to work so closely with our clients that we find their pain points and work to dissolve them.

According to a 2016 article published by the World Economic Forum, HR departments have become increasingly administrative over the last decade. It's because of this retreat of HR into the safe territory of rule, processes and policy making that companies have lost empathy for its employees. It can also explain the general consensus by most employees that neither HR nor their company cares for them.

The World Economic Forum also suggests that putting process before people can lead to a deficit of inspiration. I would add there is a deficit in engagement as well when processes or policy take precedence. Inspiration and engagement are two core fundamentals for the NakedHR professional. We pride ourselves in being the catalyst for change in our organizations, not the champions for only policies and processes.

F- hiding behind POLICY

I cannot put into words the vile feelings I have when I hear someone in my profession say, "According to policy" or "Policy states". It's almost like a nuclear explosion erupts in my head and manifests itself on my face. I typically have to count to ten before responding and even then my response is usually laced with acidic language.

I guess part of my guttural reaction comes from how many times those types of statements were said to me by someone in HR when I was a manager in the business. As a manager, I had shit to do and decisions to make but often worked for firms dominated by an HR department afraid of its own shadow. Rather than looking at a situation and determining the best course of action for the firm, employee and me, HR typically regurgitated some policy as the reason we could not do this or that. It nearly drove me mad.

When someone tries to quote policy to me, I instantly deduce they have an inability to claim responsibility for a decision. Saying that an inanimate object dictates a course of action tells me you are too scared to think for yourself and would rather be chicken-shit and hide behind a policy.

Before all of my traditional HR peeps get their panties in a wad, I am not advocating throwing policy out of the window and letting the asylum take over. I am simply challenging all of us to take ownership for any decision they make. Rather than hiding behind verbiage invoking the all-powerful POLICY, use this situation to think through the situation with a business mindset. After all, the first step in becoming a NakedHR professional is to know your business and become entrenched in it. If that has been done, you should be more willing and able to make business sound decisions without the need to quote from the good book of policy.

You don't have to live according to policy to be great

The textbook company that embodies this is Netflix. Patty McCord, the renowned Chief of HR for Netflix during its evolutionary years, is known for her business savvy approach to the talent sector of a company. In an article for HBR.org in 2014, McCord discussed the break from the traditional HR mantra of Policy and Processes:

Over the years we learned that if we asked people to rely on logic and common sense instead of on formal policies, most of the time we would get better results, and at lower cost. If you're careful to hire people who will put the company's interests first, who understand and support the desire for a high-performance workplace, 97% of your employees will do the right thing. Most companies spend endless time and money writing and enforcing HR policies to deal with problems the other 3% might cause. Instead, we tried really hard to not hire those people, and we let them go if it turned out we'd made a hiring mistake.

When Netflix launched, it had your standard paid-time-off policy (PTO). Netflix later modified this policy to an honor system where employees simply kept track of their own time and informed their managers when time would be taken. When the company went public, it completely broke tradition by telling employees they could take whatever time they felt needed. Managers and employees were empowered to work the logistics out on their own. The firm provided guidelines but not a policy.

Traditional HR thought would shriek at the thought of creating such a loose policy and moreover actually trusting employees and managers to self-regulate. As if a deregulated paid-time-off policy wasn't enough, McCord and Netflix departed from a formal travel and expense policy as well. Rather than a ten-page document of dos and don'ts, the firm released a five-word policy, "Act in Netflix's best interests". Both of these moves sent a powerful message to the employees of Netflix.

The first message was one of trust in the employee's moral compass and judgement. Oftentimes, policies are created by legal and HR teams to manage out the bad 10% of the organization. Netflix refocused its efforts to the front end of the employee funnel by only hiring those they felt they could trust and would perform. Employees who feel the company trusts their judgements are usually more responsible and prudent. Although Netflix did put in place safeguards to ensure these policies were not taken advantage of, McCord states they found the PTO and expense policies were rarely abused because the firm took the time to provide a clear expectation of responsible behavior.

The second message Netflix gave its employees was one of empowerment. I love the quote by Steve Jobs that says:

"It doesn't make sense to hire smart people and tell them what to do; we hire smart people so they can tell us what to do."

Too many companies spend a lot of time and money recruiting the top talent in their space and then once they are hired, they throw a two-ton book of policies on their backs. Netflix's policy overhaul empowered employees and made them owners. This approach to policy and processes is counterintuitive to most U.S. companies' approach to business.

According to the Harvard Business Review, U.S. Companies waste more than $3 trillion every year on excessive bureaucracy and management. That number is roughly 17 percent of the country's GDP wasted on useless and unprofitable policies and procedures. The traditional "top-down" corporate decision making and communication structure is belaboring companies' ability to be nimble enough to respond to market trends and sustain profits.

How to realign your organization

Although traditional HR departments enjoy the safety in only creating policies and procedures, the business minded NakedHR professional understands the need to streamline processes and policies to empower the employee base to grow the organization. NakedHR professionals are, by nature, so entrenched with their client and understand the business needs that the idea of spending ions working on policies to dictate every aspect of life is counterproductive.

According to Entrepreneur.com's article "4 Ways to Guide Your Employees Toward Empowered Decisions", one of the first steps toward a more productive workplace that values people over processes is to modernize the company. The fast paced economy requires companies to be swift and agile. Traditional firms with several layers of management cannot respond as quickly to market changes like those firms who have a less structured organization. Empowering employees by providing clear expectations and outlining the company objectives allows employees to act more like owners and less like kindergarteners in school.

Creating this culture is even more important considering the vast majority of job-seekers are millennials who when surveyed, stated they are more satisfied with an inclusive and creative work culture. In the same survey, only 28 percent felt their organizations were taking full advantage of their skills. We have to be the voice of reason in the room when our organizations want to spend more time talking about policies and processes than about how we can maximize the talents of everyone in the organization.

Rather than creating a thick policy handbook or a detailed chart of the required processes to accomplish something in HR, employees should be provided a decision framework. This framework can be the basis of most every decision within the firm and will accomplish several goals if implemented correctly.

- **The obvious is empowerment**. Employees who are empowered to make even the most mundane decisions tend to protect the company's interest and can act quickly. In comparison, in an organization that has multi-layered decision approval processes or lengthy policy outlines hinder employees from being able to respond to clients' needs, market changes or other vital KPIs as quickly as needed.

- **More time on acting and less time discussing.** The decision framework also diminishes the need for committee meetings and other wasteful uses of time and resources. I have found in firms I have worked with that had this type of decision framework, the conversations had between employees and managers became less about asking permission and more about the decision making process. Managers became coaches, not just hall monitors.

- **You train leaders in every aspect of the organization.** One of the core principles I have when I lead a team is to rarely provide an answer. (I do the same with my daughter.). My goal is not to be elusive but to ask questions to guide them through the decision making process. This accomplishes two goals. First, it helps me understand their thought process and gives me ideas on how to further develop them. Second, it lessens the amount of time I spend making decisions because through this process, I have had the opportunity to train my team to make decisions. The ultimate goal is for my team to feel empowered enough to make decisions that they know I would agree with.

To me, the traditional HR approach is more like a well-disguised dictatorship that assumes employees do not have the common sense to function so they should be told what to do. It uses policies and complicated processes as a form of entrapment to weed out bad performers while gutting the productivity of the high performers.

The NakedHR approach is to have frameworks of how things should be done, understanding the best ideas most often come from the employees. People are at the center of the organization, not on the periphery and definitely not seen as a necessary evil that needs to be managed by policy and processes.

CHAPTER 3

Fake and Unapproachable

Deadly Sin: HR is fake and unapproachable!

Once upon a time, there was an emperor obsessed with owning and flaunting the most expensive clothes. His obsession for wearing the trendiest clothing lines was known far and wide, attracting only the top designers to his court. Many would draw incredibly detailed renderings of their garment ideas to present to the emperor, hoping to have the opportunity to showcase their talent at one of his grand events.

When he would commission a project, money was no object. The designers could buy the most expensive material, hire the top talent in the market, all with no budget oversite. It was a designer's dream.

The only downside to such an opportunity was if the garments did not satisfy the emperor's fashion eye. There were rumors the garments that did not meet his high ideal were thrown in the royal trash and their designers, as well as their teams, were thrown in the royal dungeon. Despite this risk, designers still sought out the opportunity.

The emperor's court had become accustomed to his lavish spending on clothing and the extravagant parties he threw when he had a new outfit. Little was said publicly out of fear of retribution but many were bothered by the attention to detail the emperor had when it involved fashion and the lack of attention he had for kingdom affairs. The weight of the governing the nation fell on the court while the emperor focused on decorating himself and the palace with only the finest furnishings.

One day, a con-man posed as an illustrious designer while in the emperor's court. He promised to make a garment that would be the talk for centuries. He would use only the finest linen that was technologically enhanced to be lightweight and invisible to anyone who was unfit to be in the presence of the emperor.

The emperor could hardly contain his excitement. He commissioned the posing designer to create this magnificent garment and immediately began planning the most extravagant event to reveal his new garment to his subjects. He worked with the palace communication team to ensure everyone in the land and surrounding kingdoms knew of the upcoming event.

Only days later, the designer was ready to fit the royal in his new garment. Only a handful of the court was invited to the initial showing. When he entered with his new state of the art garment, those in the viewing room tried to hide their shock. Rather than the typical, flamboyant attire, it appeared the king was naked. Despite the obvious lack of clothing, no one dared tell the king he was naked because they remembered the designer's promise that only those loyal to the emperor would be able to see the garment.

So the emperor flaunted his outfit before the full court in an unprecedented gala and then in a parade throughout the kingdom. While he thought he was garnished in the finest linen, he was naked. Unfortunately, no one in his kingdom had the audacity to tell him.

Survey says: Fake and Unapproachable

Much like the emperor, many HR departments are so involved in a self-created reality that the employees we are here to serve deem us as fake and unapproachable. While HR departments champion themselves as the advocate for their internal clients, a 2005 survey by Hay Group revealed some damning views of HR:

- Only 40% of employees commended their company for keeping high performers
- Only 41% agreed performance evaluations and the processes involved in them were fair
- 58% rated their job training as fair.
- Most indicated they either didn't know who their HR person was or they did not have any defined opportunities for advancement within the firm

I would imagine if you were to ask some HR groups to rate themselves, the percentages would be double than those listed above. Why? Well, I guess there's a bad case of *the Emperor Syndrome!* We're not looking at the real data, only the data that supports our reality.

When I conducted a non-scientific survey asking my network to describe HR, the majority of responses could be summarized as fake and unapproachable. One respondent compared their HR department to high school cheerleaders,

> *"They're great at pep rallies and football games but let's face it, when you go to either of those events, you're going for another reason, not to see the cheerleaders."*

Another individual compared their HR department to the internal police.

> *"The only time you see them is when shit is about to hit the fan. They provide no strategic value because they don't know the business, only HR."*

FastCo's article in 2005 entitled "Why We Hate HR" says most businesspeople feel HR people are not the "Sharpest tacks in the box". It states HR departments tend to avoid hiring a lot of independent thinkers, settling for exiles from the corporate mainstream. Essentially, in the eyes of many, HR represents a low-risk career parking spot.

A SHRM survey asked HR professionals what were the most valuable academic courses to take to become successful in the industry. Shockingly, 83% said classes in interpersonal communications were extremely valuable, followed by employment law and business ethics. Only 35% responded courses in change management were valuable and only 32% valued strategic management. Other business courses like finance, accounting and other similar courses only ranked at 2%.

I wish I could say I was shocked.

There have been several times in my career when I have had clients say something along the lines of, "I forget you're in HR sometimes." This is a compliment in my opinion because I work hard to position myself as a partner who just happens to deal in the talent arena. The first 90 days I work with a new client is spent developing a relationship and learning about their business, not touting my vast HR knowledge. When I speak to clients, I tend to use their vernacular not the HR language most of my peers enjoy using. My sole goal is for my clients to see me first as a business-minded coach and then as an HR professional.

In order for HR to reposition itself as part of the business and not the cheerleader or police of the organization, it must first fix one critical issue I've noticed in clients I've worked with and organizations I have worked for-the structure of most HR departments.

Why HR departments are staffed Ass-Backwards

If you were to look at how most HR departments are staffed, you most likely see the following:

1. 2% Recruiting
2. 45% Operations
3. 50% Staff to handle Employee Relation issues
4. 3% Management/Strategic

Unfortunately, most would look at this spread and think, "Wow, we're efficient."

I look at that spread and think, "Wow, you really have that ass-backwards!"

I realize that one of the core functions of HR is to mitigate risk. It is a *CORE* function but it is not the *ONLY* function. Too many companies spend so many resources and money managing out poor or misaligned talent and mitigating risk but if they were to put more emphasis and resources on how employees enter the company, they could see a number of benefits.

Recruiting, the Last Thought for Resources but first Thought for the whipping post.

In my experience, every company I have worked with/for say it values recruiting but the structure, support and resources do not support it. Recruiters are often overlooked, underpaid and undervalued yet charged with selling the company's brand and opportunities. The praise and glory tends to go to the HR professionals who keep the ship running and away from the rocky shores of litigation. Don't get me wrong, these are important functions of HR but shouldn't we be more focused on how to avoid such catastrophes before they happen?

It seems that when things go wrong, the spotlight is placed on recruiting with question like:

- Why did we hire that person?

- Why can't you fill roles quick enough? I mean I know we are not paying what the market is paying and hiring managers are taking forever to get back to you but you're hired to be a magician! Work your magic!

- Oh, our onboarding is awful. The recruiting group should really get on that and fix it in their free time of filling jobs, marketing our brand and all while carrying a 25+ job load.

Might sound cynical but it's often the truth. Maybe your firm does not have this type of regard for recruiting but most recruiters I speak with feel the same pains. Little support given relative to the expectations placed on them.

The Solution? Beef up your Recruiting Team and lessen the HR Police.

The facts stare us in the face but organizations are slow to move resources to address it:

If recruiting teams are staffed appropriately to truly be brand engineers, talent agents, and company guards, HR partners could focus more on being strategic and valuable and less on employee relations issues and risk mitigation.

The best way to avoid having to terminate employees is to redirect energy to hiring the right ones. Ensuring success will require companies to get leadership and management invested in improving the hiring process.

The How-to:

Step 1: Change the mindset within HR

Leaders within HR must lead the charge and prioritize resources to the front of the employee funnel rather than the end. This not only includes increasing recruiting staff with the right type of people (brand engineers, hunters etc., not just paper pushers) but also includes diverting resources to sourcing the right candidates, developing a robust branding campaign and an effective interviewing routine to only let the good apples in the basket. Although costs to do this type of activity might cause your HR budget to be in the red initially, do not lose sight of the goal which is only letting the good people in your organization. Over time, the P&Ls will right size once your firm starts hiring the top talent in the market.

Step 2: Give Recruiters the Key to the Gates

Once you have the right recruiting team in place, empower them to be the gatekeepers to your organization. Challenge them to be incredibly selective in who they let "sit at your table". Give them the power and authority to be like Gandalf in The Lord of the Rings who boldly stood against a fiery enemy and proclaimed: You shall not pass! Once you give them that power, you will be amazed at how protective your newly empowered recruiting team will be of your organization. (I would also suspect their engagement will increase proportionally.)

Step 3: Educate your Internal Clients

We all know there is a cost associated with turnover, both voluntary and involuntary. We tend to only focus on one of these and it's different in every organization. In my opinion, both can be traced back to the hiring process. Once you institute this new way of working in HR, track the expenses throughout the employee lifecycle to help prove to your internal clients that your strategy is working. Within a year, you should be able to show a decrease in turnover for employees hired within the last year. If you are able, track the revenue per FTE to help show the impact of retention of new hires as well.

In most medium to large organizations, HR is the last to adapt to the changing environment. We tend to like our traditions and processes. I hope that anyone reading this takes the time to flip the employee funnel around and track the progress it has to the company's bottom line, engagement and other key performance indicators. If anything, wouldn't it be nice to spend more time and energy on how we can bring awesome people into our organization rather than how the hell we're going to get the bad ones out? I think that'd be a great organization to work for.... but that's just me.

HR needs to be data driven

One way to create value is to measure your worth. One firm I worked for had an internal mantra within HR of "lead with data". Business owners and leaders use data daily to measure output, performance and efficiency. This is their native tongue so if you want to create a relationship and be seen as a valuable partner, you have to speak the language.

Many HR professionals may feel they don't have access to the type of data that would strengthen the relationship with business leaders because they do not recognize the gold mine of information they have access to. Think about the type of data that is readily available to be analyzed within HR:

- Recruiting data
- Training data
- Demographic data
- Exit survey data
- Career progression
- Retention
- Revenue per FTE

There are a number of firms that have come to market specifically designed to measure everything talent related. Visier, one such firm I've worked with, has real time data modeling with predictive analysis on turnover and market trends. As if the data analytics weren't enough, the product even puts the information into trendy charts, graphs and infographics exportable to PowerPoint slides.

The era of big data and analytics is booming right now and an easy way for the more traditional HR departments to relinquish their image of fake, unapproachable and of no value is to lead with data. Rather than allocating time, effort and resources to the administrative tasks and legal issues, NakedHR professionals should spend more time in the data to understand what is going on in their client's shops.

Instead of simply presenting a turnover percentage, find out what is causing this turnover and where you have the most exposure. If a business unit is unable to meet its production goals, use data to determine if there's a skill gap in the workforce. When your company decides to explore new products or services, use data to provide intel on the talent in the industry and develop a proactive plan of attraction.

Honestly, HR firms that do not use data as a way to differentiate themselves will become obsolete in the next five to ten years or maybe sooner. We must become fluent in the language our clients use to ensure we prove our value and continue to have a seat at the table.

Become Approachable

In order for an HR professional to be a consultant, they first have to be approachable. I recognize delicate balance between being a coach and being a best friend that can be hard to manage for most in our profession. When I hear HR professionals complain about not having a seat at the table with their clients or not receiving information in a timely manner, I almost always assume it is because their partner does not feel they can be trusted or they feel their partner is just unapproachable.

Rather than being that friend no one wants to invite to the party, position yourself as the first person on the list. I am not saying you have to be the wild crazy friend everyone wants there to liven the party but you definitely should be the one they want to invite because you bring value.

Take a self-assessment of your approachability. Here are some questions to ask yourself:

1. When you get ideas or suggestions from your client, do you shut them down immediately or do you acknowledge them in a thankful tone?

2. Do you take time to explain your reasoning or line of questioning rather than simply going in for the kill?

3. Do you "show up" only to execute initiatives or are you present for other events as well?

4. Have you taken the time to get to know your client on a personal level or do you keep it strictly business?

It takes time to shed the stuffy, uncomfortable business attire and become a NakedHR professional. Honestly, when I first began my career in the industry I thought I had to be well-guarded and the know-it-all. I have thankfully found my own balance over time and feel I am more approachable than most in my field. There are times I still struggle with what I call the "stoic HR" persona but I have also taken time to develop a group of accountability partners to keep me in check.

If you work for or with an HR department deemed unapproachable, understand it will not change overnight. As mentioned in previous chapters, the industry has retrenched itself to the safe place of administration, control and compliance over the last two decades.

3 Easy Rules to Change Perception

In 2015, I began working for a new director who I affectionately refer to as my work mom. We shared a similar background in that we both came from other departments to HR so we usually approached HR issues with a more client centric lens versus the traditional HR focus. Over time, she saw my internal struggle and began to coach me how to be comfortable in my own skin and find my voice. (Sometimes I think she may have regretted it though.)

In one particular situation, I was struggling to find the best communication method to a project team. The project was super frustrating because of the leader's communication style and personality, further complicated by a lot of internal politics. She knew from our one on one coaching times these two types of problems tended to send me into a world of freak out and internal struggle. The real me wanted to showcase the nuclear explosion going off in my head while the "HR" me tried to keep things cool, calm and collected while sugar coating my communication. That's when she shared with me the three rules I now live by. *Be real, be raw, but be respectful.*

Be Real

I think the lack of authenticity is not just an HR problem. Although the tide is slowly changing, I believe there are still many organizations that spend too much time dancing around subjects versus being direct and real. One of the core principles of NakedHR is to be naked which means no hiding, no covering up, just being you.

Confession. This was a long and difficult process for me. There were times when I went too real and times when I didn't feel I had the courage to be real enough. It's still a battle for me sometimes but I have learned that when I am real with people, there are numerous benefits including:

- An increase in productivity because more time is spent on identifying obstacles and opportunities versus determining the correct verbiage to use or putting on a façade.
- It allows me to deepen the relationship with my clients and their employees. Once I set the tone for authenticity, it becomes reciprocal and there is a development of mutual trust in the process. An increase in trust most certainly leads to a deeper relationship.
- It has helped me recognize failures quickly, admit them and begin the learning process. When we wear a mask, failures get hidden for the sake of pride. Being real forces you and the other party to admit the failure but not dwell on it. This leads to a shorter time period between the

failure and the learning/growth phase.

Be Raw

So if being real sounds tough, being raw is going to be even harder. Raw is defined as natural, unrefined and crude. How does this translate to the NakedHR principles?

First, it's ok to say something sucks and not feel guilty about it. Furthermore, it's even more important to be raw in your communication style with your clients, especially when confronted with a tough or sensitive matter. Hiding emotions or mincing words during such situations only causes internal frustrations which may cause you to lose your focus, overlook important details and/or make a wrong decision. All are recipes for disaster.

As mentioned before, I tend to ask permission before going raw if it is the first time I have worked with someone. A simple, "Can I be frank?" or "I need to be blunt about something" can prepare the other participant for what's about to be said. Most times, after being raw and getting whatever it is out of my head and on the table, I am able to think more clearly and address the needed behaviors decisions etc. that led the client to the situation we are dealing with.

It's not fun to do but it is liberating and effective. A NakedHR professional is not always the cheerleader, sometimes we have to be the coach that grabs the player by the facemasks and asks them, "what the .... Are you thinking?"

Be Respectful

It may sound contradictory to have this as one of the rules considering the previous two but it is necessary. Being real and raw should never give someone the right to degrade the other person. You can identify the stupid actions or processes that led you to the conversation without calling the other person stupid, idiotic or a moron. (Even though sometimes you want to.)

Also, being real and raw with your clients is a form of respect. You are showing them your concern for them as a human first by removing any masks or "pretty" language. Your honesty and authenticity will reinforce your first priority is their well-being and growth.

I know the irony in using a fable about a naked emperor and comparing them to the faults of traditional HR. It can seem a little oxymoronic on the surface but there is a point to the fable and my decision to use it.

So let's amend the story to have a NakedHR ending. We'll pick up when the king walks into court wearing his new getup.

So the king, in love with his new outfit and devilishly excited to debut it to his court, bursts into the room flaunting his perceived 8th wonder of the world. As he walked through the court, he became acutely aware of the facial expressions of his leadership team as they gazed upon his elegance.

"Wow, this is not the reaction I thought I would receive" he thought to himself.

So rather than continuing his walk down the runway, he opened the floor for feedback.

"What the hell do you think you're wearing? I can see every roll in your stomach!" said one of his advisors.

"Honestly sir, I don't think you should go out in public wearing that or not wearing that actually," said another.

One by one, each of the court leaders shared their feedback to the emperor. The emperor listened intently to the raw candor and began to see the error of his ways. He realized he was there to serve the people and had not been doing a great job of that lately.

After a quick change into some real clothes, the emperor made a proclamation. He had been inspired by the NAKED outfit and made a vow to become a better emperor. Everyone lived happily ever after.

Ok, it's not that easy but hopefully you get the point. Let's turn the tide of public opinion of HR and start being seen as approachable, authentic and invaluable.

CHAPTER 4

HR, You've Lost that Loving Feeling

Deadly sin: HR only protects the business and doesn't
care about its people.

Confession, this has been the hardest chapter to work on. I've tried writing it at least ten different times to include some move reference or story but all efforts have been unsuccessful. I believe the hardest part in writing this chapter is that I have no cognitive empathy. In my mind, HR is there to protect the business's people which ultimately protects the business. I have found through some conversations with participants this is not true in most organizations. So, this will most likely be the shortest chapter!

A Brief History of HR's De-Evolution

The modern Human Resources function has its origins in the late 19th century when companies needed a department to allocate workers (resources) on the assembly lines to produce products. In the early 1900s, companies became focused on how to reduce turnover and maximize performance which evolved the personnel departments into HR-1.0. This version of HR would conduct exit interviews and provide management the data. Although it sounds as though the companies were interested in the data to retain great employees, it was more about how to keep unions out. According to Peter Cappelli, professor of management at the Wharton School and the director of the Center for Human Resources, "By the 1930s human resources started to become and be seen as advocates for employees and the reason for that, frankly, was because companies were trying to keep unions out."

It was the introduction of workplace regulations including EEOC, Civil Rights Acts and others in the latter half of the 20th century that caused a shift into more of the HR we know today. Added to the list of responsibilities now included employee relations, managing risks, benefits, onboarding and much more. To further complicate the true focus of HR, the Supreme Court mandated in 1998 employees seeking legal recourse would have to first file harassment complaints with the HR departments. HR was tasked as the gatekeeper and the mandate forced the industry to become more of a compliance and risk cop versus a department to represent and advocate for the employees of a firm.

It is understandable how any HR professional can have conflicted allegiances. In small to medium sized companies, HR executives usually report directly to the CEO and have more day to day interaction with the C-Suite than it does with the employees. Even in the larger corporations, HR professionals tend to work more with executive and middle management than the employees who report to them. I can see how many of us would naturally align ourselves more with the executives whose primary focus and responsibility is to protect the organization.

There is an inherent danger with this unbalanced alignment. Here's an example.

Susan Fowler, a first time engineer at Uber, most likely joined the firm with the hope of joining Uber's mission to transform the world. Uber is one of those "sexy" firms to have on your resume, much like Google, Facebook and others, applicants seek to join these firms because of their trailblazing product development, exposure to cutting edge technology, and the bragging rights associated with this type of experience. Unfortunately, Susan found herself receiving inappropriate chats from her male manager. When she presented documentation to HR, she was informed she should find another team or stay in her current position and risk a negative performance review.

Susan began a blog once she left Uber, sharing her experience and exposing the numerous times HR failed her as an employee. Uber launched a massive internal investigation which eventually led to the termination of 20 employees. The firm's investigation noted numerous cases of negligence by HR professionals eager to protect high performers versus regular employees. So why did Uber's HR department do nothing to protect Fowler and what does this say about the true role of HR in any organization?

It doesn't just happen at Uber and it's not always a drastic incident that causes a lack of faith in HR as an employee advocate.

I spoke with an employee recently who described his interactions with HR. He shared with me his journey with an organization as one of their top performers. A typical trait of high performers is their desire for continuous feedback and a challenge to continuously improve. He tried talking to his manager about advancing his career but his manager told him to consult HR. When he approached his HR partner for feedback, he received none.

His next interaction with HR was in the form of applying for roles. Although his firm made a commitment to internal promotions, roles he applied for were filled with external candidates who did not have the qualifications he possessed. He received no direction or feedback from anyone in HR regarding his interests in the roles.

Again. Radio silence.

The final interaction with HR was on a video conference with his colleagues informing them their positions would be eliminated. They announced the firm's intentions to outsource the department as a business decision. There was no admittance of care or concern, merely a reading of the basics of the severance agreement that would be offered. When I asked him his thoughts on HR after his interactions he used one word: Sterile.

There were several similar stories of HR failing the employee to protect the business. While I understand the need to be tactical in handling tense situations, we should never lose sight that humans drive the organization. Without our employees, there would be no need for us. I have to believe there is a balance between protecting both the employees and the business.

I worked for one firm whose HR director did not like my approach to handling severances. In 2007, I had the unfortunate responsibility of laying off several employees who worked for our operations groups. I began each meeting with my sentiments on the duty I had to execute. I can remember standing in front of roughly 50 employees at one of our centers in an open area to make the announcement. I had thought carefully about what I was going to say, following legal's advice but it all changed when I saw the faces in the room. I saw their humanity and acted accordingly.

"This part of my job sucks. It sucks not only because of what I have to do but also because I can empathize with what you will have to go through. I've been on the other side of this table before. I hope you know that this decision has nothing to do with you as a person and how we value you as an individual. It has everything to do with the tough decisions businesses sometimes have to make. We value you and will do everything we can to help you land on your feet. So with that, let me do this thing that sucks."

I was "counseled" later by one of the Senior Vice Presidents in HR who questioned my loyalty. I believe the phrase she used included, "I'm concerned whether you have the best interests of the company as your guide". WTF? As my guide? When I asked her why she questioned my loyalty, she informed me that my job was to deliver the news and hand out the packets, not admit any fault. She felt by empathizing with the plight of the employees, I put the company in jeopardy.

I'm happy to say that not one person filed any lawsuit as a result of my speech. In fact, many thanked me for being delicate and being real. It did not change the outcome of the decision to take away their job, but it did let them leave with some dignity. My job was to protect them and the company and honestly, I wouldn't change a damn thing about how I handled it. Those affected by the decision understood the business need but I hope they also recognized I did everything I could to protect their self-worth in the process.

HR as the Nervous System of the Organization

I have yet to meet someone who did not marvel at the wonders of the human body. Billions of cells working together behind the scenes to manufacture life in countless forms of beauty and wonder. As a self-proclaimed nerd, I immerse myself in documentaries, books, and articles related to the inner-workings of our bodies, especially anything to do with the brain. The contrast of complexity and simplicity that serves as the basis for life is both amazing and inspiring to me.

For example, have you ever considered the nerve cell? The human body has over 100 billion nerve cells responsible for transmitting billions of messages to and from the brain. Neurons in the brain are connected to form an amazing network allowing synapses to flow through it, alerting us to pain, joy, fear, hunger, thirst and a million other types of messages. According to an article in ScienceDaily.com in 2015, nerve cells interact much like a complex social media network.

Nerve cells form a bewildering meshwork of connections called synapses -- up to several thousand per cell. Yet not all synaptic connections are equal. The overwhelming majority of connections are weak, and cells make only very few strong links. "We wanted to see if there are rules that explain how neurons connect in complex networks comprising millions of neurons," says Professor Thomas Mrsic-Flogel, the leader of the research team from the Biozentrum (University of Basel) and UCL (University College London). "It turns out that one of the rules is quite simple. Like-minded neurons are strongly coupled, while neurons that behave very differently from each other connect weakly or not at all."

The same nerve cell that can trigger a message to the brain indicating pain can also send a message of comfort or warmth. And although these neurons in the brain have millions of connections, the strongest bonds, according to the research above, are shared with like-minded neurons. But what about the weak bonds? Dr. Lee Cossell, one of the authors of the study, believes the weak bonds represent the opportunity for learning.

"If neurons need to change their behavior, weak connections are already in place to be strengthened, perhaps ensuring rapid plasticity in the brain."

He goes on to say this plasticity allows us to learn and quickly adapt to our surroundings. So even in the weakest of bonds, our brains have the ability to take information received to grow, adapt and learn.

One of the ways you can employ the NakedHR process and avoid the deadly sin of protecting the business instead of its people is to think of HR as the central nervous system of the organization. We should take the cliché of having our "finger on the pulse" and transform it to mean we *become* the pulse. We should embrace the idea of having stronger bonds with our like-minded counterparts, usually management and executive level employees, while also maintaining the bonds to the weaker connections (or the employees) as a way to measure every synapse happening in the organization.

Think about how amazing it would be if we could become that conduit of communication throughout the body of our organization. Immersing ourselves in the business, as we discussed in previous chapters, would allow us to know our employees on a more personal level, opening our "nerve network" to messages that may have gone unheard before. These once weak connections would allow us to learn more, be more innovative and help the organization become nimbler.

We Must Evolve

Human resources has to be one of the greatest bait-and-switch professions one can join today. HR departments position themselves with a forward-facing fluffy image, whether improving the productivity of workers through training and development programs or perhaps righting the yawning inequality gap in America by encouraging diverse hiring standards. Unsurprisingly, the field often attracts starry-eyed idealists, people who seek a mission-oriented, perhaps even noble profession for their careers. They join thinking they are going to make a difference. Then the corruption happens.

Danny Circhton, Tech Crunch, Februrary 2018

In my heart, I believe all of us joined the HR profession with the goal of changing the world. As Circhton mentioned above, HR departments position themselves as the energy of the organizations and the empowerment of every employee it serves. We do a great job bringing employees in and selling them on how awesome the company is and will be the cheerleaders present when there's a company event. Unfortunately, in most organizations, those are the two happiest times employees interact with HR. There is radio silence until the shit hits the fan and HR needs to become the judge, jury and executioner. This lack of engagement consistency can leave most feeling as though HR is the great protector of the company and not the "little people" it was originally designed to represent.

To further complicate the matter, most medium to large companies see HR as a necessary evil and do not invest the resources needed to allow the department to maximize its potential. I have worked in some atmospheres where the department was cut to the very bone but expected to deliver unreachable deliverables while keeping a positive attitude. The work and responsibility was overwhelming, especially for someone like me who is wired to entrench themselves in the business, making connections with not only managers but the employees as well. There were several nights I worried I just did not have enough in me to fully live up to what I felt the employees in the firm deserved: an engaged, involved and focused HR partner.

While overworked and undervalued, we tend to become cynical and miserable in our roles. We look down on any new idea that might add to the long list of laborious tasks thrown on us. We develop a cynical view of smaller companies or startups that offer employees new perks or resources as a way to increase retention. The phrase, "That would never work here" needs to be replaced with "How could we do that here?"

The evolution to NakedHR will require a lot of work and refocus, but it will be worth it. Employees everywhere want to feel as though they have an advocate they can trust who will be invested as much in them as they are the company. Both the business and the employee should see a positive ROI of their time and resources. We will discuss the "How To's" in the chapters toward the end of the book or as I like to refer to them: The NakedHR Makeover. We have to evolve to let our employees know we haven't lost our loving feeling, we've just been a little side-tracked.

See, I told you it would be a short chapter!

CHAPTER 5

·My Name is No

Deadly Sin: Not consultative, always tell you know "No". AKA HR does not add value

Not too long ago Meghan Trainor released the song entitled my name is no. As I started thinking about this chapter, that was the first song that came to mind. In the song she basically repeats herself saying her name is no her answer is no etc. If you think about, it I may feel this should be the ringtone when HR calls them. In fact, while speaking with one of my clients recently, I mentioned this idea and they chuckled. The laugh itself was enough of an indication to me that they agreed with the sentiment but were too embarrassed to let me know.

No "Option 2"

Have you ever tried calling customer service for a major company and been so frustrated with the process that you choose not to do business with them anymore? Let me tell you about a recent experience that I had that made me do just that.

I had some personal finance business that I needed to take care of so I called my financial institution. So rather than talking to a human, I had to go through a list of at least nine different options before I could get to where I could speak to a representative. The process took roughly 5 minutes for me to even try to talk to a real person. As if that were not frustrating enough, by the time I got off hold to speak to a representative, the call was disconnected. Inside of my head, there was a nuclear blast of frustration.

To make matters worse this happened at least two more times! Needless to say that after the third time I decided this was not a company I wanted to do business with. I began looking for alternatives and found a small, local credit union. I called the branch, spoke with one representative who made an appointment for me to come in that day.

From the time I walked in the door to the time that I walked out with money in hand was 45 minutes. Within the next 48 hours I moved all of my finances to the small credit union based on that one interaction.

Although I did not have someone verbally telling me NO, whenever I was calling into the phone tree at the big financial institution, every time I got disconnected or ran into any point of frustration I felt as if someone was screaming NO!

Unfortunately, employees who interact with HR do not have the option to go to a "competitor HR department". They are simply stuck with whomever answers the phone, assuming that someone actually does pick up the phone. Honestly, this is a huge source of frustration for most employees in any organization. Do you need some examples?

- I'd like to terminate a problem employee. *HR*: No, you don't have enough documentation.
- I'd like to give my top employee a raise to retain them. *HR*: No, you have to wait until merit increases or No, that's beyond what our policy allows.
- I'd like to reorganize my group to be a bit more efficient. *HR*: No, you lack the authority to make those types of changes.

I know that some of the feedback and I will get on this subject will be from long-standing HR professionals who say that their first job is to mitigate risk. I do not disagree completely with that statement but I do think that there is room for us to help our clients grow.

In July 2016, a blog post on the SHRM website outlined why HR professionals should be more like consultants and less like the stuffy, "shut them down" bores of HR past. Here's the passage:

HR must support every department within the organization. At the same time, HR is increasingly being recognized as a strategic partner within the organization. Business leaders and executives are turning to HR for input on organizational strategy. One reason for this shift is their realization that the organization's human capital—its people—can quite literally make or break its success, both short- and long-term. And when leaders in an organization start talking about people, what is the first department they should think of?

Although the article was written in 2016, the wave of consultative age of HR has yet to catch on or go mainstream. One way firms can begin this transformation process within their HR department is to begin actually bringing people and from what most businesses called the line of business. An example of this would be bringing in a strategic manager in the firm into the HR department to help lead this transformation process. The successful leader will be able to learn HR fairly quickly, leverage the centers of expertise within HR, while also teaching those within the department more of the business mindset.

A Lesson from Tech Startups

In the tech world, the Design Thinking methodology has redefined the development process. Rather than the traditional view of "Build it and they will come", developers, stakeholders and product owners meet in the design phase with one question to answer: what does our client want?

The Nielson Norman Group wrote an article outlining the principles of Design Thinking and outline the stages as empathize, define, ideate, prototype, test and implement. Recently, I had the opportunity to participate in a weeklong Design Thinking class held specifically for the HR team of a firm.

During the class, we spent a lot of our time on the first stage discussing tools, methodology and ideas on how HR could empathize with its clients. It was interesting to see how many in the room were astounded by this "new" concept. Imagine the thought of actually empathizing with your client as an HR professional. (Please understand that sentence is laced with sarcasm.)

As the design thinking methodology was implemented in the firm, I noticed a mindset shift within 60 percent of the department. Rather than simply unleashing a new policy, the firm's HR department began leveraging feedback sessions with the employees to be affected. There were several iterations of the "product" before it was released to the entire employee base.

This is a consultative approach to HR. Rather than simply going into any situation as if you have all of the answers, seek first to understand. Sure, most of the time we have a general idea of what the proper solution for most situations are but take some time to learn more about your client in the process. There may be industry trends or other internal issues that you would miss if you go into the meeting guns blazing with an "HR knows it all" attitude.

Furthermore, the idea of bringing in outside resources (as in outside of HR) into the department can help shortcut the empathize stage of design thinking. I have found those of us who are used to working with clients tend to more empathy for our internal client than those who have only had an HR job. The natural tendency is to see the client more as a partner than an adversary and usually have better results working through difficult situations.

Get to Yes

Despite my tendency to go rogue in comparison to some of my fellow HR professionals, I still find myself hesitant to say yes to everything a client wants to do. Let's face it, there are some things we just can't advise our clients to do. So how do you break the perception most have about HR as the NO Department?

Option 1-Use No, but...

When I am consulting with a client, I have to admit that sometimes my first answer is NO. Over time, I have learned to force myself to say "no but". Here's an example:

> *Manager*: I want to terminate this person because they have come in late for the last three days. Can I?
> *Me*: I understand how frustrating it is to have someone consistently come in late, the short answer is no but there are a couple of alternatives.

See how different it sounds? I'm still accomplishing the task of protecting the company from a potentially bad decision; however, I'm also offering a solution.

On my team there is a strict rule that I enforce which I affectionately call NBR or the NO BUT RULE. Rather than simply telling someone NO, team members are required to offer a solution and an explanation as to why the short answer is no. All too often, HR professionals do not take the time to educate clients on wide decisions are potentially dangerous. They just simply tell them no.

Option 2- Ask for clarification

Rather than simply saying no, ask your client what they hope to accomplish. This allows them to pause and examine the problem they are attempting to solve rather than merely focusing on the solution they desire.

Option 3- Ask for alternative solutions

Remember, the goal in these situations is to coach the manager/ client how to think for themselves through these scenarios. The thought process to find an alternative solution allows you to say no without really having to say it. I have found in many instances; my client will actually fall more in love with their alternative solution than the one they called to get me to buy into. This works best because the alternatives are usually smarter and better for all involved. It's also best when it's their idea to own and implement.

Saying no is easy but can ruin your relationship with your client. There is a happy medium between being the king or queen of "NOville" and being a "Yes Door Mat". Everyone has to find their own comfort level so start today with small steps to embrace your new journey as a NakedHR professional.

CHAPTER 6

Stop with the F### Political Correct-ness

Deadly sin: They're so politically correct, I don't know what they're saying and I don't know what I can say to them.

Let's talk more about the more traditional HR professional. I alluded to an example of this in an earlier chapter where there are certain types of HR professionals who seem to only know how to speak corporate language or politically correct (PC) verbiage. They are the ones who are so hypersensitive to how things are perceived in society, they tend to overlook basic logic and basic business sense. These are the type of Consultants who give the rest of us a bad name. And this chapter is specifically for those types of Consultants!

When I began research for this book, 1 had a number of stories from people within my network of HR gone wrong. One of them struck me as particularly disturbing but not because of the circumstance, more of how the HR reaction made this person feel.

I will paraphrase this participant's story below:

I began with my company two years ago and love what I do. I am a young, white male who has been openly gay for four years. I choose not to be flamboyant about my lifestyle but I do not hide it either.

Over time, I began feeling threatened by some of my peers and some managers. I work in a very manly environment so I do tend to stick out of the crowd when conversations come to football, hunting and other topics of the like.

There were two instances when either comments or suggestive language had been used with me by members of management. At first, I thought it was a bad attempt to be funny but over time, I realized these were down low advances. When I did not return the advance or attempted to draw clear lines of professional relationships, things got uncomfortable for me. There were comments, office events I was not invited to and advancement opportunities I was not afforded.

I spoke with my HR department regarding the issue to ask for some guidance and intervention. During the first meeting, the HR professional confessed they did not know I was gay-as if that had any relevance to my intent to meet with them. I was told that it would be hard to prove any type of sexual harassment since I was gay and those I was accusing were married with children.

Since that meeting, I have felt isolated and unprotected in a company that I thought I wanted to work for. I can't help but to think that if I were a woman, things would have been addressed since that is more Politically Correct than a gay male being subjected to harassment by straight males in the office.

Honestly, when I read that, I was speechless and angry. This was one of five such stories I received as part of my research and the only way I could categorize them was PC malpractice. The HR department allowed the popular PC topic of the day to deny someone the opportunity to feel human and valued.

I also received most feedback from managers who said HR was more concerned about being politically correct then about actually running the business. I know from my own personal experience as an HR consultant there are times where I have to mitigate risk depending on how a particular decision may impact the business but this should not come across to any of my clients as me being more politically correct than business-savvy.

HBR.org released an article in September of 2006 entitled "Rethinking Political Correctness" addressing this very topic. One quote in particular caught my attention:

Despite this obvious progress, we believe that political correctness is a double-edged sword. While it has helped many traditionally underrepresented employees to experience their workplace as more inclusive, the PC rule book can hinder employees' ability to develop effective relationships across potentially divisive group differences. Companies need to equip workers with skills—not rules—for building these relationships.

Traditional HR tends to go for the flavor of the day whenever it comes to PC. Even as an HR professional, it's incredibly difficult for me to keep up with what is and is not politically correct. The example shared with me above seems to indicate that the HR department only classifies a situation as sexual harassment whenever the male is the aggressor against a female. I believe all of us can agree that there are many forms of sexual harassment and all of it is intolerable. Unfortunately when you only focus on the hot topic of the day, you may overlook other items that need to be addressed.

Let me be clear, I do not advocate the careless speech or disregard for humanity like we've seen with celebrities Matt Lauer, Bill O'Reilly and countless others, including a sitting president. The type of NakedHR I like to promote is an environment where everyone is free to speak about whatever is on their mind using whatever language they need to convey their thoughts and feelings in a respectful way. In order for this to be effective, politically correct terminology has to have a place. But how do you do this and still honor everyone's feelings?

In today's hyper-sensitive environment, it is incredibly tough to have a naked conversation with anyone since everyone seems to be wearing their feelings on their shoulders. Language barriers caused by our PC culture has become borderline absurd and a metaphoric wall to growth and development.

I've had several instances where I had to lead a conversation that was incredibly PC charged. My goal for the meetings, keeping in line with naked HR principles, was for everyone to be able to speak freely by informing participants of my ground rules: be raw, be real, and be respectful.

PC mania is counterproductive to encouraging high functioning and high performing relationships in the workplace. As a NakedHR professional, your role is to be the catalyst for deepening relationships with your clients and teaching them how to do the same with their employees. Constructive engagement of the differences that make us unique requires you to develop a mindset that nurtures differences and propels the organization to success.

In the same HBR.org article listed above, the author suggests applying some insights classic diversity-related dilemmas, we have developed the following principles to guide managers and employees seeking a healthy way to alleviate tensions that commonly associated with differences:

- Pause to short-circuit the emotion and reflect.
- Connect with others in ways that affirm the importance of relationships.
- Question yourself to help identify your blind spots and discover what makes you defensive.
- Get genuine support that doesn't necessarily validate your point of view but, rather, helps you gain a broader

perspective.

- Shift your mindset from "You need to change" to "What can I change?"

These principles can help facilitate a healthy dialogue among employees and foster new ideas and deeper relationships. Unfortunately, too many traditional HR professionals jump to the common antidote of sensitivity training or some other canned approach to diagnosing the problem. In my opinion, this is not only malpractice but really nullifies the reason why an organization would pay someone to be in HR. Our jobs are to lead fearlessly into areas of with landmines to help bring understanding and productivity. Sending someone to a class or doing a group Kumbaya session only cheapens the emotions experienced by the team and makes diversity another item for employees and managers to just check of a list of to-dos. This approach forgoes the opportunity to create a more dynamic, productive and connected team.

When I speak to managers for the first time, I can often tell the hesitation in their voice when they are explaining a "hot topic" employee issue. They tend to skirt around potentially important details in an effort to avoid stepping over the proverbial PC line of accepted behavior or speech. At some point in the conversation, I will stop the manager and remind them of the HR/Manager confidentiality agreement and that I am there to be their partner, not their adversary. The NakedHR professional has ensured they differentiate themselves from the traditional HR police mentality to foster growth.

Political Correctness Paralysis

In November 2007, Valda Ford wrote an article for the SHRM blog entitled, "The Paralysis of Political Correctness." Her posts gave the example of a physician client she was working with who was asked to speak at a conference. His biggest pain point was not the subject, location or how he was to speak to the crowd but more like what to call the niche group: Hispanics or Latinos. She uses the story to highlight how many of us become paralyzed over common sense issues involving any of the hot PC topics including race, gender, sexual preference and religion.

Ford defines paralysis of political correctness as:

- The fear that keeps us from communicating in culturally and linguistically awkward situations.
- The fear of using sensitive words or communications because they might embarrass or hurt the sender or receiver.
- That tongue-tied, stomach-churning sensation that makes us avoid those employees who may need us the most.

According to Ford, PC Paralysis usually stems from fear in one or all of the following areas:

1. Lack of knowledge
2. Regulatory and administrative retaliation
3. Lack of Competence
4. Any of the above being discovered

This group of fears can easily be addressed by a NakedHR pro. Sure, there are great group exercises, reading materials and training out there to leverage but I have found an open, heart to heart conversation with someone accomplishes a lot more. Sometimes the first step in addressing a fear is admitting you have it and naming it. Sounds like part of the 12 step program for addition but we must understand our fears can be equally as crippling.

I guess for me; this PC paralysis rarely takes hold because I grew up in a very diverse environment. Although my family has very closed minded tendencies, I was fortunate to be a minority in a number of the schools I attended from kindergarten through high school. It created in me a curiosity and fascination about other cultures and points of view that is still a part of me today.

While in middle and high school I went to largely African American schools. As such, most of my friends were African American which was difficult growing up in a southern town in Alabama. I listened to popular rap music, enjoyed the Black History Month and was a keynote speaker in my senior year for the Martin Luther King celebration. In fact, while in high school, I held the esteemed position of "Minority Representative" on the student council. Yeah, think about that. A white guy holding a minority position in a majority black school but I was representing 10% of the school's population of white.

The interesting thing about my upbringing is that during this time, most of my friends and I would talk openly about stereotypes for both races. We asked each other questions to help understand what was true and false. During my middle and high school years, racial tensions were high with Rodney King and OJ Simpson topping the news stories of the day. Rather than these topics becoming divisive, my friends and I used it as an opportunity to speak openly about our feelings and through this raw, real and respectful exchange, I feel we learned more about tolerance. We didn't know it at the time but we were living the Franklin Covey principle of "Seek first to understand then be understood." (Actually, St. Francis was the first to provide that nugget of wisdom-just clearing the record.)

Fast forward some years and that's how I like to approach highly charged, PC related issues. Rather than acting like Chicken Little and screaming the sky is falling, I prefer to be more rational and seek to understand both sides of the matter before making any judgement. For my clients, I walk them through the same exercise I learned early in school by facilitating one on one or group discussions around difficult topics with the goal to create understanding through raw, real and respectful communication.

Rules of Engagement-How to put PC in its place

Here are a couple of steps to help you embrace the NakedHR principles related to managing PC in the office.

Step 1: Identify your own fears

Remember the first rule of NakedHR is to be naked right? Success in any endeavor starts with you so you must address your fears first before attempting to help others. Are there topics you flinch at when they are brought to you for help? If so, educate yourself in those areas first. Of course all of us still have areas we feel we need to tiptoe through because of a lack of knowledge or exposure. These instances present the best opportunities for growth through candid conversation with others.

You can start by opening the kimono with a fellow HR professional, friend or family member to discuss your fears. I have found that when I speak the fears aloud, I either realize how stupid some of them sound or I learn more how to deal with them through wise counsel from the conversation's participant. You're an HR professional, not a know-it-all so address your fears and move forward.

Step 2: Take every conflict as a way to expand healthy dialogue

The fear of PC diminishes as people learn more and expand their understanding through raw, real and respectful dialogue. You should be the first to suggest this course of action when PC related events are thrown at you. As the facilitator, don't forget to be naked with your fears regarding the subject as well. I have found that admitting my own shortcomings can open the dialogue and allows participants to see me more as someone seeking knowledge than just a cheerleader facilitator.

Step 3: Don't let it go

The worst thing any HR professional can do is to simply let the topic go and hope it goes away. NakedHR professionals are wired to be decisive when it comes to addressing hard topics so take on the situation quickly. Also, while you are handling the issue, do not be afraid to drill down past the incentive words or actions that caused the situation. You will need to play the role of warrior, mediator and psychologist in most scenarios related to PC. Don't be afraid to keep prodding until you are certain the root of the issue has been dealt with and monitor the situation later to be sure there are no other issues lurking below the surface.

Step 4: Create the environment for others to grow

NakedHR professionals must serve as the catalyst for growth in their organizations and PC situations are not immune to this. You have to be the champion for diversity of thought as much as diversity of the more common areas like race, creed etc. How do you do it? It's easier than you think and can be rather fun. Here are a couple of quick ideas:

- Celebrate the various cultures in your organization through corporate events. They could be a lunch and learn or inviting members of a particular group to share something with the company about their culture through cooking a meal, showcasing art or anything else to encourage open dialogue.

- Create a culture council in your organization that is representative of the diversity on your teams to help champion open dialogue. You don't have to do this all on your own! The best ideas usually come from groups like these who are passionate about harmony in the organization as well as education as a weapon against ignorance.

Those are just two ideas but there are a number of companies like Erikson and Google who have championed the PC topics most organizations stay away from. Do some research and determine which ideas are best for your organization and beta test them before going all out. This will help you determine the best ways to be the Warrior NakedHR professional who refuses to let PC paralyze them, their employees or their organization!

A rant about diversity

It wasn't too long ago when my daughter made a comment to me that made me pause: "Dad, you have the most diverse group of friends you know?"

Looking back over my life, I realized my circle of friends and acquaintances were always diverse. I am not just speaking about racial diversity but cultural, religious, thought and more.

I guess I like learning about other cultures? *No that's not it.*

Maybe I like being "that guy" who's the true representation of the new cultural ideal called "inclusion"? *No, that's not it either.*

As I have spent some time really trying to understand the "why", I realized I was making it too complicated. The answer is simple, I love people and enjoy understanding what makes them tick.

I guess what drives me nuts is how this topic has become about checking boxes or embracing change when it is really about people. When did we take the HUMAN out of humanity? I do not understand why I should have to train anyone to look at someone for WHO they are and overlook WHAT they are. Sure, I see someone's race or nationality, but that does not define who they are and better yet, who they could be in my organization.

So am I passionate about diversity because it's the "in thing"? Absolutely not.

Is it because it's part of my management responsibilities for my current organization? Hell no!

I'm in it to win it when it comes to Diversity because I want to change the conversation. I want us to start talking about humanity and not just diversity. I want to sit with managers and candidates to learn how they would fit in this human puzzle we call an organization. And by fit, I don't mean do we have a group for them to fit into but do we have an opportunity that aligns with their passion and skill set? If we have that, what else really matters?

We need to start having those difficult conversations but be able to have them in a safe environment. If there are no female leaders in your organization, you should be able to have that conversation with the management team and understand the reason why. Perhaps it's because they have a bias or perhaps it's because your recruiting strategy sucks. Either way, the conversation needs to be had. When deeply dividing events happen nationally, we have to pull our teams together and talk through the feelings in a safe environment. We have to start listening to each other again with not just our ears out of obligation but our hearts out of necessity.

To end, I would like to share another story about my little girl.

Part of my Christmas gift for her in 2015 was a trip to Atlanta. While there, she and I visited the civil rights museum in Atlanta. It is a memory I will not soon forget.

As we progressed through the museum, we had to stop often because her emotions took over. I remember standing on the second floor in the middle of one of the exhibits, holding my daughter while she cried. Her heart's pain made me find myself holding back tears as I tried to console her.

Later in the journey through this troubling part of history, she sat and watched a film showing countless acts of inhumanity. Again, she got upset and looked at me with a face of pure confusion. Once she regained her composure she asked, "Dad, how can someone hate someone else so much that they do this kind of stuff?"

It was one of those times as a parent when I didn't have the answer. Honestly, I ask myself the same question. Why can't we see each other as humans who make up a beautiful, delicately woven and divinely made fabric?

So to answer the question, my passion for diversity and keeping PC in its place is driven by my daughter. I want her to be raised to see that people are not defined by what they are but who they are. I want her to know that one person can start a revolution and affect their organization which will affect their community and the families within that community. One decision to be passionate about the human experience and bring compassion, understanding and fearless communication can affect generations if we just take the first step.

"I hope that we become a lot less hypocritical once we realize we all have a skeleton and massive flaws." Gary Vee, Chain X Change Keynote

CHAPTER 7

Tear down those walls

Deadly Sin: HR is too political and has too many silos.

I love the character Dory in Disney's Nemo and in her own movie Dory. She's a beautiful surgeonfish who has some minor memory issues. It seems she can recall long-term memory but tends to forget anything her friends tell her only minutes before. As one could imagine, this can present a major problem if you're trying to save your friend's son Nemo or find your parents at an aquarium.

In her second movie Finding Dory, the forgetful fish is determined to find her family. In one scene, she is given directions through a complicated maze of pipes within the aquarium that would take her to the majestic tank where her parents are thought to be. Not long into her journey through the winding pipes she begins to forget the directions to her destination. As anxiety overwhelms her, Dory begins to swim in circles until her friends use the pipes to communicate step by step instructions to her final destination.

The complicated politics and silos residing in many HR departments can leave employees feeling a lot like poor Dory. We tend to forget that most employees do not daily operate in our complicated world so when they have to venture down some winding maze of pipes known as HR, they tend to have the same reaction as Dory: anxiety, fear and ultimately mental shut-down.

First, let's define silos using the Business Dictionary: a mindset present when certain departments or sectors do not wish to share information with others in the same company. Unlike many of the business terms that have been around for more than twenty years, the "silo problem" still seems to be a cancer that has permeated every department within most companies. It seems though that HR is one of the departments most employees perceive as incredibly siloed and unproductive.

In David Forman's book Fearless HR- Driving Business Results, he asserts HR can modernize only after it lets go of its complicated past. He goes on to state that most HR organizations are too soloed and inwardly focused. In the 2016 Connecting with Impact Survey of 500 HR leaders, nearly two-thirds of the respondents agreed the silos within HR were a detriment to their company.

So why are internal politics and silos still a problem?

Many executives view their departments as their little kingdoms. They are the heads of state and those reporting to them are serfs carrying out the mission they design. The executives

86

tend to dismiss interdepartmental inefficiencies and further encourage a silo mentality within their organization. These silos become internal political wars that wage among the executives and trickle down into every facet of their departments.

One would think that HR is to be the department to break these silos but my experience discounts that idea. I do not have enough time to tell the countless stories of either working in an HR department or consulting an HR department where the evidence of politics and silos were not present. This department doesn't like that department so they don't interact without a specific mandate from the CEO. This HR group believes the focus should be on one area while the other group feels another initiative should be focused on. On and on the battles rage while employees who seek answers get lost in the turf wars.

AGILE-It isn't just for tech companies

One antidote to this plague is the concept of AGILE. The concept of AGILE working has been around for decades but has recently gained exposure with the rise of the tech startups. Companies large and small have begun adopting this mindset to increase interdepartmental communications as well as creating a more sustainable product. If you were to Google "Agile software development", you would see over 14 million results.

The common business challenges today include improving time to market, inspiring continuous learning, increasing responsiveness and collaboration according to the Harvard Business Review in its June 2017 article on the subject.

The Agile manifesto released in 2001 has evolved to become a business methodology rather than simply a way to develop software. The general principles of the Agile Method are:

- Satisfy the client by providing a product designed specifically for them through a continuous development cycle.
- Developers and business people must work together throughout the entire project.
- Projects are completed by participants who exist in an environment conducive for growth, communication and support.
- Self-organized teams usually produce the best results.
- At regular intervals, the interdisciplinary teams should meet to provide updates on the status of the project and adjust the production schedules accordingly.
- The teams are to also meet bi weekly to perform a retrospective to identify lessons learned and obstacles to the project schedule.

The dependency of interdepartmental communication and ownership is key to the success of the Agile methodology. Agile teams are able to work not only independently but also interdependent to accomplish a common goal. There are very little hierarchies within an Agile team so everyone is an owner in the wins and losses of the project.

Since 2012, "Agile HR" (Deloitte) has become a popular term to describe the new age dawning in the HR profession. The days of each HR department head creating their own kingdoms and not playing with others has begun eroding in small and large organizations as they adopt this methodology. Deloitte defined the goal of Agile HR as empowering HR to better "manage volatility, enhance adaptability and strengthen the organization."

Sounds like how we've defined a NakedHR professional thus far right?

In traditional HR management styles, the focus was execution, order and control by implementing policies, standards and systems to drive alignment and execution. Agile HR departments are more focused on adaptability, innovation and speed. They tend to define success more as the ability to implement programs, systems, strategies which foster expertise, collaboration and decision-making.

Redesigning the traditional HR to a more Agile mindset can ignite a change that will allow HR to become nimbler and open to the changes in the businesses they support. Let's research a couple of ways Agile methodologies can influence key areas within HR departments.

Silo Objectives versus Unified Missions

Traditional HR usually loves its job descriptions or as I like to call them, the job handcuffs. The requirements define compensation and whether one candidate is better than the other. Such an approach could potentially cause a firm to miss out on a talent who has the aptitude to become a high performer on a team simply because they lack one or two of the requirements.

Agile HR views jobs in how they support the mission and values of the organization. Performance and training is provided in short iterations to mirror the iterations within a project.

Reactive Recruiting versus Continuous Talent Acquisition

In the old world, talent management and acquisition is owned by HR so searching for talent begins only when a position is available. Once the best candidate is identified and hired, the talent acquisition process is complete.

Agile HR encourages the organization to develop a dynamic employer brand and identify methods to cultivate relationships with potential talent without a job being open. The goal becomes to identify the talent then create a role within the company versus the other way around.

HR is the system of record versus HR as the system of engagement and deployment.

We have discussed the numerous examples of how traditional HR organizations love their policies, procedures and processes. Their main objective is to mitigate risk and track any issues. The success of such departments is measured by documentation and output.

The Agile HR organization is more focused on aligning itself with the business and engaging the employees within that unit to accomplish business goals. The Agile HR professional (NakedHR professional) measures success in terms of employee retention, increased satisfaction levels, innovation and achievement of the business goals, not just HR's.

Projects move laterally within HR versus Projects have interdepartmental members.

Projects will begin at the executive level and will be assigned to one department or a group of departments that will work on their pieces independently. Progress is defined as meeting timelines and departmental objectives before moving the project to the next group according to a waterfall project mentality. Allegiance is to the department and not the project.

In the new world, projects begin with an interdisciplinary group that defines the scope, deliverables and importance. Project teams work cohesively within the project to accomplish the goal. The team members are representative of their departments and serve as subject matter experts, not turf warriors. Allegiances is to the successful completion of the project, not to the supremacy of their department.

Going AGILE

According to a KPMG research conducted in 2014, 60 percent of company's leaders expect HR to grow to become more strategic and provide value leveraging this strategic ability. The same study found only 17 percent of the same leaders felt HR did a good job demonstrating its value to the business.

For HR to become more Agile, it must accomplish three tasks outlined by David C. Forman in his 2016 post to the Talent Management and HR blog. These tasks are:

#1. HR must give itself the chance to break from the chains of the past. Change is hard and most times, the biggest obstacle to change is releasing yourself from the past. HR leaders must lead the charge to redefine what HR will be while acknowledging the deficits it has allowed in the past. If done correctly, this can be a rallying call for all within the department to transform into NakedHR professionals

#2. HR professionals must either possess or acquire new skills and capabilities to perform at the strategic level. Traditional HR organizations are typically subject matter experts in only one area-HR. To transform the division into more a strategic, business savvy organization, there may be a need for training on subjects like data analysis, financial statement comprehension and consultative skills. Leaders should find ways to provide this training to all levels within HR to ensure the tools needed to provide strategic value are present.

#3. HR must believe in its own capability to transform and develop itself into the Agile organization. Every college student who has taken Psych 101 knows of the self-fulfilling prophecy which states a when we believe in a prediction, it may directly or indirectly cause it to come true. Leaders, middle management and even entry level HR employees must believe they are capable of transforming to become a value to the organization.

These three steps are the first to be taken when removing silos and adopting a more agile work environment. Luckily, if your organization is considering making this move, you do not have to recreate the wheel. Several notable organizations have already undergone massive transformations for you to learn from.

ING is a perfect example of an established organization that transformed itself by going agile. In January 2017, two senior executives from ING were interviewed for McKinsey Quarterly about this transformation. The transformation began the summer of 2015 comprising of roughly 350 nine-person "squads" in 13 "tribes". This approach has already improved the firm's time to market, employee engagement and productivity.

The two executives interviewed discussed the before and after of their people model. In their old organization, the manager status and compensation was based on the size of the projects as well as the number of employees. (Sound familiar?). The new agile organization redefines the performance-management model to place more value on how people deal with knowledge. This forced ING to restructure itself based on the need to have a good mix between layers of knowledge and expertise.

Transforming into a no silo and less political structure was not easy. ING's transformation included all employees at headquarters being placed on a "mobility" status and had to reapply for a position in the new organization. The selection process placed higher weighting for culture and mindset versus knowledge and experience. The result was nearly 40 percent of the employees were placed into different positions, more aligned with their mind-set.

Choose your story

Whether you choose to go agile or not, you have to consider how you can remove the perception that politics and silos rule HR. For most of the organizations I have consulted with in the past, we didn't necessarily "go agile", rather, we focused on ways we could create better communication and diminish the territorial nature within the department. Sometimes this meant having difficult conversations with members of HR regarding their mindset and in many cases, it means some members of the department being encouraged to find another opportunity.

NakedHR has no room for politics or silos. We are more focused on removing any obstacle to move the company towards its objects and profit, even if it means cleaning our own house first.

CHAPTER 8

The NakedHR Makeover

One night in the fall of 2013 I did something I had not done in a long time, I stood naked in front of the bathroom mirror. I had been avoiding it for the last two years because I knew I had gained weight and I guess by not looking in the mirror I somehow convinced myself it wasn't as bad as I thought it was. But that night, I faced reality. Not only was did I weigh in at 258 pounds, but my waistline had gone from a size 32 to 36 (even though I really should have been in a size 38).

I hated what I saw. I was 35 at the time but looked older. I didn't sleep well, lacked self-confidence and had little or no discipline in my life. The man looking back at me was not the man I wanted to be. I had rolls hanging over my hips. My pecs were disguised by fat yielding to the pull of gravitation. There were dark circles under my eyes and I had lost my neck in the process of gaining weight. I was genuinely embarrassed by my appearance.

That night was a turning point. I decided it was time to get myself back to the weight of 200 where I had spent most of my life but more importantly, decided to do it for my total health, not just vanity.

I enlisted the help of my best friend Matt who was a personal trainer to design an eating plan and workout to help me shed the pounds. The first month was a brutal war between my mind and body. As I forced myself to retrain my brain to think of food as fuel, I slowly embraced the idea of being the out of shape guy in the gym.

Matt also required me to send him progress pics as a form of accountability since we were in different cities. I reluctantly agreed but the process of taking the pictures was grueling for me. Once a month I had to give myself a pep talk to stand in front of the mirror in my boxers and document my progress. Although Matt always saw positive changes, I still saw the fat, depressed man looking back at me.

I was determined to accomplish my goal and change my mindset so I did something that terrified me. I posted my progress pictures on Facebook. As painful as it was to post pictures of myself, I found the accountability motivating and as time went on, I began to see changes which added to my motivation.

Fast forward five years and I weigh in around 194 pounds and have a decent physique. People will usually comment on the change in my appearance if they haven't seen me in a while, but in my mind, there's still a fat and out of shape guy looking back at me in the mirror. When I tested book cover ideas for this book, I took pictures in only my boxers against a white screen with an idea to have a banner with the book's title covering my private areas as a way to add a shock value to my marketing campaign. When I looked at the pictures, I noticed my pecs were still sagging, my midsection didn't have the six pack I wanted and my legs were still undeveloped. Regardless, I used the picture in my prelaunch campaigns. Why? Because I still have to force myself to be naked-real, unaltered and unafraid.

So why the long story about my fitness journey? It isn't to boast on my weight change or share my body image issues but to show you that embracing NakedHR will make you uncomfortable and it will be a journey. It will force you to face some things about your career and your style of HR that might make you embarrassed but I want to challenge you to push through it and keep your goal at the top of your mind.

I still have a picture of the body I want to have and that's my goal every morning when I go to work out. It's my accountability reminder when I want to gorge myself on ice cream or French Fries. When I look at myself in the mirror, I notice the positive and negative changes in my body and use it as fuel to make the necessary changes to achieve my ultimate goal. You must do the same! If you have embraced the portrait of the NakedHR professional I outlined in the previous chapters, create some type of goal in your mind or on paper to consistently compare yourself to.

Remember, this is going to be a marathon, not a sprint. Take your time, focus first on the changes you need to make before trying to change your HR organization, especially if you're in a medium to large sized business. If you make the changes to become more like a NakedHR professional, you'll begin to garner the support and partnership of your clients which will help you make the changes you need to in your HR organization.

The HR departments referenced in this book are known for hiring, firing and risk management. Sure, there may be additional items done by your HR department but the perception by our internal clients remains unchanged. If you read this book, you have learned how using the NakedHR principles, you can change how your internal clients view your role. I'd also like to think that you'd be a hell of a lot happier as well.

This section of the book is your roadmap to overcoming the 7 Deadly Sins and transforming into a NakedHR partner. Remember, this will be a slow process regardless of the size of your company. The evolution of HR will take focus, determination and a lot of courage but I'm here to help you with this playbook.

The Makeover Process

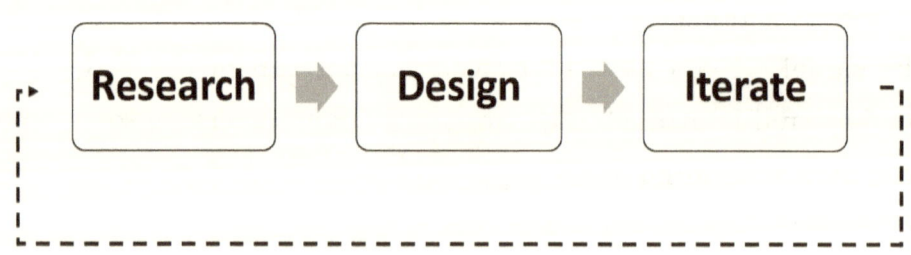

You'll notice what I am suggesting is not complicated but it is continuous. The needs of the business are the core of the

NakedHR Makeover. In the next sections, I plan to go through each one of these steps in depth and provide ideas as well as case studies where this process has worked.

Research

In Mike Michalowicz's book, "Clockwork", he introduces the QBR or Queen Bee Role. He compares well-functioning companies to a beehive. The queen is no more important than the other bees but her function within the hive is critical. "Each bee in the colony knows it needs to do just two things, in the same order, every time. First, each bee must ensure that the queen bee is protected ... then, and only then, the bees go do their primary job [producing food]," he wrote.

Michalowicz defines the QBR as the core function you decide to hinge your company's success on. Defining your NakedHR QBR can only be done when you know what your company's QBR. To accomplish this, you will need to immerse yourself in as many functions of the business as you can manage. This phase has the following goals:

1. Understand the QBR of your business by immersion
2. Understand how the employees in your organization serve the QBR
3. Define your QBR to support #1 and #2

Immersion

Immersion is best done by job shadowing as many levels in the organization as you can. Learn how managers run their units by using spending the day as a tag along. Your role is to observe and ask questions to gain insight but be careful not to appear as though you are part of the Spanish Inquisition. Try allotting a portion of time with the top performers in each area to understand what makes them top performers. If you have a sales department, go out on client visits with them and learn what your external clients need from your organization.

When I worked for a large financial institution, I spent time with the sales group by going on calls with them. I enjoyed meeting clients and hearing firsthand how the services we provided were sold but I enjoyed the car ride with the sales agents more. Those rides allowed me to talk with the employees and learn what their obstacles, perceptions, needs, and fears were. Listening to the interactions with our clients and the sales pitch helped me understand more what our true value proposition was. All of this information became the framework I made every decision while supporting the division as their HR partner.

The next step would be attending team meetings as often as you can. This allows you to dive deeper to see not only team dynamics but also a 360-degree view of the opportunities and threats in the market. Asking questions during the meeting will not only help you gain a deeper understanding of the business but will also show your partners you are engaged in solving their problems. Use this time to truly connect with your units on a deeper level. Your ultimate goal is to shift the perception that HR is a cost center to a profit-enabling center.

Aligning yourself with the business goals is one of the final steps. Now that you have a more hands-on understanding of how the business works based on the time you spent out of the HR Ivory Tower, you understand the levers employees need to pull to make your company profitable. So when the business comes to you with an issue related to the talent in the organization, you'll be better equipped to search for solutions that will enable the talent in your organization to accomplish the business goals. You have to transition from the single focused HR partner to more of a business-minded consultant.

If you are not currently entrenched in your business, problems or projects presented to you are viewed in only one lens: HR. During your rotation in the business, you should be able to answer the following questions:

How does your business make money?

You should understand how each department in your organization works to either make, protect or grow money. You should also be able to understand how each of the business units work together and rely on one another to make money.

What are the positions or job families that most impact the bottom line?

I have found knowing the answer to this question helps me identify the positions executive management will always want to see data on including but not limited to hiring, retention, performance, pay against the market and tenure.

What are the most profitable products or services you manufacture?

Profit is king so if you understand the products/services that make the company the most money, you'll be able to anticipate certain decisions as your company evolves through the business life cycle. You will also be able to prioritize your focus when it comes to projects, hiring, and engagement. Although the units producing these goods should not be your only focus, they should demand a bit more of your time.

Who is your biggest competition and why?

Your goal is to take this answer and develop retention strategies so your top performers aren't lured over. Understanding why a company is deemed your biggest competitor should go deeper than just talent. You should understand how they compete. Is it price, market share, a more superior product or others reasons? Each will have different impacts to your talent plan. If they compete on price, then you should determine if somehow your "cost of people" is too high or if perhaps your people are affecting the efficiency in the production of your product. If their market dominance is based on marketing, find ways to enable your talent base to out maneuver them by providing some additional sales training or other solutions. Find the top three reasons and dedicate some time to providing a plan and solutions to help your business units gain market share.

What are the top 3 market trends that keep your people up at night?

This is one of my favorite questions to ask my clients: what keeps you up at night. The answers range from hitting a production goal to people issues on their team to concerns about the industry. Dig deep and gather a good list. Using this list to develop your HR plan will not only be a way you can have an immediate impact but also a way to show your business leaders you were listening.

What do the financials tell you?

Most HR people shrink away from anything regarding financials unless it pertains to budgets. I'm challenging you to go deeper and have an understanding of trends in the financials, even down to a basic department level. Financial knowledge is critical for you to be able to do the following:

1. Understanding the business's operating cycle.
2. Making financially sound decisions.
3. Controlling working capital.
4. Monitoring cash flow.
5. Managing corporate resources.
6. Improving bottom-line results.

Strategic Finance Magazine addressed the need for HR and Finance to be closely aligned in an article it released in June of 2016. Here's an excerpt:

Under the traditional business model, employees were often considered an expense. The cost of salaries, benefits, hiring, and firing received much more attention than the critical contributions that employees made to the company. Now, as companies better recognize the role that employees play in business success, things like employee output, knowledge, creativity, and problem-solving are valued more highly and are seen as critical revenue-producing or profit-contributing assets.

This growing appreciation has led to an increased focus on human capital management strategies to maintain, protect, and expand employee resources. There are three significant steps you can take to align HR efforts more closely with the company's financial systems: (1) realign company strategy to incorporate improved human capital development and management, (2) develop a dynamic recruitment program that aligns with company strategy, and (3) develop new measures of success and improved employee retention systems. The result most likely will lead to increased profitability and greater business success.

NakedHR professionals know if you're in HR and you don't know your numbers and don't know your business well enough to add value, then you don't deserve a seat at the table with the big dogs. The executives in your organization speak the universal language of "numberese" so if you don't speak the same language, you will not be seen as valuable. Furthermore, the initiatives that you feel are valuable to the organization may be misaligned to the business goals.

Your goals should include the following:

- Be seen as an integral part of the success of your firm
- Position your department to have a permanent seat at the strategic table
- Be a true business partner to the operational unit you are supporting
- Be prepared, when appropriate, to question, push back and challenge the numbers like any other member of the business team.

Getting into the numbers and learning your business's financial levers will not only get a seat at the table but also align your efforts to the business goals.

Traditional HR is seen more like the police guarding the walls around the organization. They're there to ensure everyone does what he or she are supposed to and enforces the rule of the land when employees violate one of those rules. This perception perpetuates the notion that HR only values the processes and policies which leads employees to believe HR professionals are unapproachable because they will protect the business before they protect employees. Becoming entrenched in the company and knowing the financials will help begin changing this perception.

HR departments organized are typically based on a service-delivery versus a consultative model. This has forced HR departments to focus on enhancing service, reducing costs and staying efficient. As a result, HR has allowed itself to be seen as an expense unit versus the profit enabling unit it should be. According to Forbes: "Our research, which is briefly shown below, shows how HR has to be more «distributed» and «embedded» in the business. We need HR advisors and business partners to function as senior consultants, and we need specialists in HR to be intensely trained and connected."

NakedHR is an evolution to a more consultative model focused on leadership development, execution of business objectives through talent management, and branding. The NakedHR professional is focused on high-impact principles that will help drive business objectives through the talent in the organization. Here is an excellent infographic provided by Bersin by Deloitte High-Impact Principles.

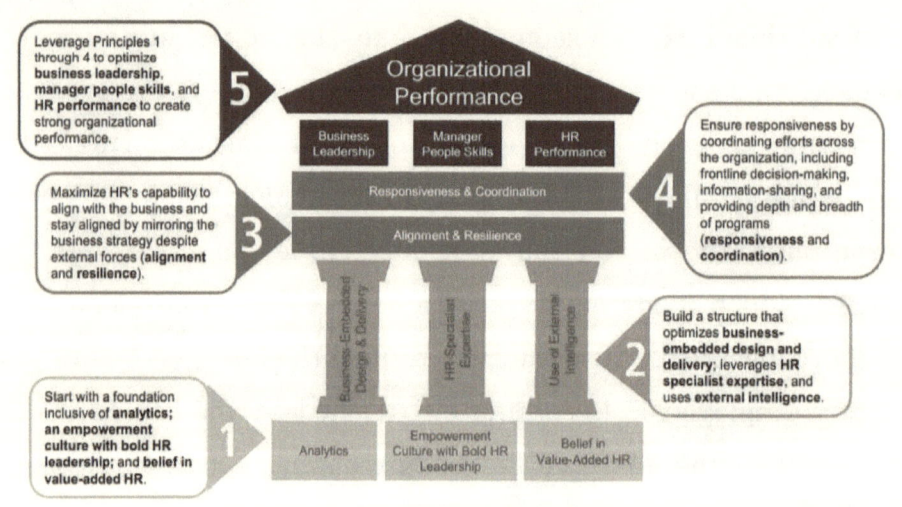

Source: Bersin by Deloitte, 201

As you can see from the figure above, the end goal is organizational performance. Building or rebuilding your HR department to be embedded in the business will drive not only the focus but also increase the expertise within your group. NakedHR professionals are dual brained, part business and part HR. They use their business knowledge along with a deeper understanding of the external forces affecting the business to make decisions and policies that have the high impact their business units want and deserve.

Next, Let's Design

In the design phase, you will take all of the information you learned from the research phase and begin developing a product and plan to meet the needs of your clients. Keeping your client at the center of this process is critical to your success as a NakedHR professional. I referenced a training I went to on Design Thinking in previous chapters but we will go more in-depth to define precisely how you can put this into practice.

Design Thinking is defined as an iterative process to understand the user, challenge assumptions, and redefine problems in an attempt to identify the right strategies and solutions to meet their needs. Although it may seem like common sense, the goal is to have the client at the center of the process and their needs ever-present in the conversation during this phase. Design Thinking provides a solution-based approach to solving problems. Do not think of it as a process or a new way of doing project work but more a way of thinking and working.

In the Design Thinking methodology, there is a process loop which we covered in Chapter 6. As a reminder, the Nielson

Norman Group outline the stages as

- Empathize-with your users (this is done in the research phase above)
- Define-the user needs, their problem and your insights
- Ideate-challenge assumptions and create ideas for innovative solutions
- Prototype-create solutions for integration testing
- Test and implement.

Empathizing

You will find shifting your mindset to the client will be more challenging than you think. During my training, I had to battle my tendency to presume I knew what was best for the client. I would have some great idea that I thought would be the answer but when my group and I would go back to our research from time spent with the client, I would realize my solution wasn't addressing the core issue. The design phase is perhaps the most frustrating because of the constant mindset shifts you have to do to retrain your brain. Go with it, embrace the frustration and know that you will be a better consultant once you go through this mental strength training.

Our instructor told a great story that showed just how trapped in our old ways of thinking can prevent us from seeing the simplest answer right in front of us.

A couple of years ago, a trucker underestimated the height of his trailer before going under a bridge on a busy highway. The misjudgment caused the driver to find himself lodged firmly under the bridge, unable to drive through or reverse out from under the bridge. Of course, this happened close to rush hour when thousands of cars would be racing home so the emergency personnel rushed to the scene to solve the problem.

One group took a more engineer-minded approach and began devising ways they could dismantle the truck as a solution. Another group determined it would be best to order additional trucks that could perhaps pull the trailer from under the bridge with brute force. And then there was a group that focused on what made the trucker think he could get under a bridge with a trailer that big- not even addressing a possible solution but rather, more focused on how the problem arose.

During this forty-five-minute deliberation, cars began to crowd not only the highway the truck was on but many of the roads leading to it. Wrecks happened in the surrounding area due to the increased traffic delays which put a strain on the emergency response teams, most of which were locked in a heated battle under a bride at the moment. Needless to say, there was at least a ten-mile radius of pure chaos surrounding the lodged trailer.

A young boy walking close around the scene listened as the various groups jockeyed for power, believing their solution was the best. He asked a straightforward question to the highly trained emergency personnel, "Why not just let the air out of the tires?" When the solution was tested, the truck crept under the bridge with little or no further damage done to the bridge or the trailer.

Does this sound familiar? As issues unfold in organizations, spend more time looking for the simple, innovative solution to the problem rather than trying to make things more complicated than they need to be. One of the biggest complaints I hear from employees and managers is how convoluted HR processes can be (remember the chapter on silos?). So when I sit down with my team and we use our design thinking process, I keep one quote on the whiteboard to remind us all.

"Simplicity is the ultimate form of sophistication." Leonardo da Vinci

NakedHR professionals become almost obsessed with simplicity as a way to create impact and increase efficiency and is a way to empathize with our clients. HR teams have a daunting task of supporting their business units but I think we try to make it more complicated than it needs to be with extra steps in our processes and more documentation than we need.

Some of the complexity in the industry is driven by laws and regulations that we have no control over so these are not the processes I will address in this section. The areas I want to talk about are the processes we develop to make our jobs feel essential and those that satisfy the control and command mentality traditional HR prides itself on. I want to use another method from Mike Michalowicz's book, "Clockwork" to categorize your processes: Trim, Transfer or Trash.

Trim

- Are there ways you can combine steps within the process to make it more efficient and take less time?
- What is the employee experience during this process?
- Do they (employees) question the validity of the process?
- Are there too many confusing steps?
- Are there ways to honor the process but streamline it?

Transfer

- What are the administrative processes you spend time on that can be transferred to another area of HR or be outsourced completely?
- What tasks are you unwilling to let go of more because of your sense of control versus the need for you to be the one to do them?
- What tasks divert your energy and attention from your responsibility to the firm's QBR? Identify them and transfer.

Trash

- When you examine the process, are there redundancies that should be eliminated?
- Identify processes and ask if they are needed to satisfy some law or regulation? If not, do you really need it? (If so, can you make the process easier?)
- What could you eliminate that would be a game changer for how employees view interacting with HR?

I chose to address the trim, transfer, trash method in the empathize stage because this is where you can gain some quick hits in your makeover process. Another reason to keep your mind on your customer, as well as simplicity, is that as an industry, we tend to mire even our greatest ideas with complications of our own making.

So now that you've researched your client through immersion and gained some insight and empathy, it's time to begin identifying their needs, problems and ways you can become the ultimate HR partner they deserve.

Defining

Defining the user needs and problems will be easy after you've spent time with your client in the research phase. Although you will most likely have a ton of feedback to go through, it would be wise for you to spend some time documenting each of the items in buckets or categories. Get yourself a large pack of post-it notes, find a blank wall and begin writing each of the items on a post-it note. Once you've documented all of the feedback, go through your notes on the wall to begin categorizing them. You'll find that many of them can be combined to make the daunting task of designing solutions much more manageable to accomplish. Define the pain points as either, people, process, or policy issues.

The People Category is defined as those items directly related to your clients' interactions with HR. Is there a disconnect in communication? Does your business unit feel HR is unapproachable or fake as we discussed in a previous chapter? If so, put the post-it notes in this bucket. Do the same for processes and policy-related issues.

The defining phase will be challenging but stay focused. Keep your client at the center of the discussion and avoid the tendency to define what *you* feel the issues are and stick to what the *client* says the issues are.

In design thinking, one rule shared in my training was to never fall in love with a solution. My advice to you is to put a time limit on the ideation phase not to cut off ideas but to force you to create as many as possible. Don't limit yourself to two hours of ideation to fix the more significant issues, give yourself or your team two days to thoroughly vet any possible idea that might get omitted with a shorter time limit. Challenge the team to go big with their ideas, nothing is off the table. Maybe one team member has an idea to have an avatar chat service for real-time customer service delivery to your clients. As outlandish as it might sound, write it on the board and keep going. Don't let the team focus on one particular solution until the end of the ideation phase. Keep those creative juices going.

Once you have your whiteboard full of your big, audacious ideas, begin thinking of which ones would be low-hanging fruit and tackle those first. With the remaining items, prioritize them in order of impact to the client. Which solutions would have the most positive impact on your client and position you to become more like a NakedHR department? Identify those and determine a timeline and assignment of responsibility.

Prototyping

So many HR organizations do great with the previous steps but then wholly fail with prototyping. The tendency is to create a perfect product and release it to the client but I want to challenge you to remember both the Design Thinking and AGILE methodology. Your goal is not the perfection of the product but rather, perfection by achieving what the client wants. To do this, you'll need to involve your client for feedback in every stage of development. If you plan to do a massive overhaul of your department, involve some of your loudest critics to gain insight on items you may have missed in the ideation process.

This accomplishes two primary goals. The first, you get insight from your clients' point of view. Sometimes they will find gaps you may not see because you are too close to the issue. The second goal is gaining their buy-in. Involving them in the prototyping process allows them to have some ownership in the ultimate product which will increase their buy-in as well as create some cheerleaders for you when you do release the final product. And that is how you need to define perfection.

Test your product in small pockets or single business units in your company before going live. The information you receive from this stage will be vital in further developing your idea. Be open to the criticism from your client and use it to go back to the empathize, define, and ideate phase if needed.

Iterate

In 1970, the head coach of the University of Oregon track team, Bill Bowerman, had an idea. What if he could make a shoe that would give his athletes a competitive edge? He found that many of the track shoes lacked the grip needed to give athletes sure footing while running. Consumed with the idea, he poured melted urethane into a waffle iron in the kitchen of his Eugene home in the hopes of creating a better sole for the shoes worn by his runners. The following year, the small imported-sneaker business he had started in 1964 with one of his former milers, Phil Knight, became Nike Inc.

I would imagine that if you looked at the first pairs of Nike shoes and compare them with today's shoe, there would be a lot of differences. Nike is committed to constant evolution centered around the needs of their clients. The Nike mantra for sneaker domination has its roots in Knight's famous quote: Always listen to the voice of the athlete. The Nike office has this quote extending two stories behind its reception desk in their headquarters.

Nike didn't just create a great shoe and decide to market it for forty years and expect returning customers. Remember, this process is a loop, not a straight line so there will be no definitive end. Even when you have released your final version of the product, make yourself revisit this process quarterly or yearly to ensure it retains its value. Like Nike, you have to commit yourself to be not only revolutionary but evolutionary.

An iterative process is a process for calculating the desired result using a repeated cycle of operations. An iterative process should be convergent, i.e., it should come closer to the desired result as the number of iterations increases. This may sound exhaustive but it is necessary for the NakedHR professional. Your goal is to become invaluable to your client and that will not be achieved by finding a silver bullet.

The best example of the iterative process is the use of Wikis. The content on Wikipedia is user generated so anyone is free to improve the content at any time. This crowd-sourcing approach to iteration allows Wikipedia information to remain relevant and stand the test of time. Involve your client in the iteration process and don't be afraid to allow them to modify your product through their feedback or direct access to the product design.

Keep yourself accountable to iteration by placing a pseudo-shelf-life to each product or initiative you commit to. Create a spreadsheet or project calendar with the birthday of each delivery item and celebrate by going through the design process again. This will allow your HR organization to be more client centric and avoid the 7 Deadly Sins.

The Goal

Jacob Morgan is an HR author and futurist. I follow his column on Inc.com and as a NakedHR professional, you should too. Many of his articles are in line with the topics discussed in this book. You can find more information about Jacob by visiting his website https://thefutureorganization.com. I received his blessing to use the model below as a roadmap detailing the changes needed for HR to move away from the traditional command and control function to more of the NakedHR I have outlined in this book. For the full article, be sure to go to Inc.com and search Jacob Morgan, Evolution of HR for his full article and infographic.

From Police to Consultant

Rather than HR being seen as the enforcers walking the halls of the company, the NakedHR professionals will be seen more as consultants for everything workforce related. They will have a seat at every table and their insight will be valued because of their new involvement in business operations. Their insight will be attained through daily client interaction on multiple levels, not just the typical calls to HR related to payroll, hiring or firing.

From maintaining status quo to blowing shit up

The NakedHR partner is no longer confined by the status quo. He or she is empowered to go where no HR professional has gone before with their ideas and the execution of these ideas. Their relationship with their client allows them to constantly evolve and anticipate the needs of their client. The NakedHR partner will change as the market dictates, not following the lagging evolution of traditional HR. They will get into their business, find ways to serve the QBR and blow shit up that stands in the way. They are a consultant, engineer and warrior of change.

From following strategy to leading the strategy

Long gone are the days where HR just follows the rules set by the executives in the company. The NakedHR partner has a seat at the table for a reason: they help craft and lead the strategy of the company. Their intimate knowledge of how their business units work allow them to help shape the future of the company.

From expense center to profit-maximizing center

The old HR was a drag on the budget, a necessary evil to keep the company out of trouble. The NakedHR department will be seen as a department focused on the QBR and an innovation center for profit maximizing strategies to propel the company into record profits. The tools of the NakedHR department now include financial knowledge, analytic capabilities, strong relationships with the line of business and employee experience. They are critical to the success of the business and no longer a drag on the budget.

From fake and unapproachable to valued partner

You are no longer confined to walls of the Ivory Tower of HR. Your new home is with your clients, in their business and blowing shit up. Your business units will not see you as fake and unapproachable because you've taken the time to get to know them and the businesses they lead. You've gotten naked with them (metaphorically speaking of course) and shared the real you with them. They see you more as a partner and forget you are in HR.

From siloed and broken to dynamic and innovative

Old HR loves its hierarchies and will kill to protect them.

NakedHR loves the fluidity needed to accomplish the firm's QBR so goodbye siloes. Everyone in the NakedHR department moves toward a single purpose, protect and enable the QBR. Nothing is more important, not even that corner office.

From miserable HR professional to the life of the party

Tired of being that stuffy, boring HR person that no one invites to anything? Well, get ready to be the life of the party, the center of the action, and the top invitee to all company events. Shedding that confining business suit of buttoned up boringness will be the most freeing feeling for you and those around you. Being naked allows you to spend less time trying to be what you think people want you to be and more time being the real, effing awesome NakedHR professional. Damn it'll feel amazing to go into work ready to blow some shit up, empower your clients and be a part of the journey to maximum profits.

From the out of touch department to the central nervous system

The NakedHR department will be the conduit through which communication flows in the organization. The NakedHR partner will leverage the new connection with the business units to be the pulse of the company. Feedback from employees and managers will be communicated to the executive teams to help develop growth strategies. Key business initiatives will be communicated throughout the organization by the HR team who will not be the corporate cheerleaders but the masters of engagement.

From process, policy and the business first to people first

You can't spend all this time with your business units/clients and still value policies and processes over the people you support. You'll become so entrenched in the people you support that you now balance the need to protect both the business and its people. Your people are at the center of every decision you make and it feels great!

CHAPTER 9

The NakedHR Challenge

When you think of traveling to Germany, some of the most obvious cities to visit would be Berlin or Munich. I would be surprised if anyone would have one of the lesser known but fastest growing cities in Germany,Leipzig, on their bucket list. This enchanting city has fostered historic greats including Bach, Mendelssohn, and Goethe. Its location at the center of a major trading route allowed the city to rise to prominence since the Middle Ages.

Leipzig may not as much name recognition as its sister cities, but it was Leipzig Germany that cradled the spark to ignite a historic change.

In June of 1987, President Ronald Reagan made his historic speech at the Berlin Wall, calling for Mikhail Gorbachev to open the barrier between West and East Berlin. The wall separated two opposing ideologies that arose after World War II. On the west side of the wall, citizens enjoyed a more democratic society versus the east side who suffered under the Communist regime.

Some may say Reagan's speech ignited the crumbling of both the physical and metaphoric wall but the citizens of Leipzig were the true catalysts for change. The 800-year-old church downtown had become a center for people to come to pray and discuss politics for a decade before the wall came down. Over time, the small meetings initially held at the church grew in attendance. On October 9, 1989, there were close to 8,000 people inside the church with more in the plaza calling for change.

The protests grew from Leipzig to other surrounding cities with citizens bravely protesting under the mantra, "We Are the People". Although no one knew it at the time, these demonstrations placed incredible pressure to reform and led to the fall of the wall merely five weeks later.

It was not a significant political figure who began the movement to tear down the wall, it was a group of common citizens, passionate for change who tore it down.

So why the story?

If you are reading this and find yourself a rebel in a traditional HR organization, the tasks to transform your organization can seem overwhelming. Many in your position would wait until an organizational figurehead called for change and then rally behind them but you may not have that choice.

You may have to form your own city of Leipzig within your HR department. Try to find others who share the passion you do to be a NakedHR professional and start meeting. I am not advising you to create a mutiny but rather revolutionize the way you do HR.

Understand it will take time for others in the organization to see the impact you have on your clients and use that curiosity to start tearing down some of the walls within HR.

My final encouragement and challenge to you is what I call the Furious Four. These are the top four things I tell HR professionals who are ready to get naked and up their game.

1. *Transform yourself first.* Identify which of these sins you are the guiltiest of and make a resolution to change. It will be hard and it will be scary but trust me, there is such freedom on the other side. Find an accountability partner outside of HR to help keep you on the right path and provide an outlet for your frustrations.

2. *Start small.* If you identify four areas you need to grow, don't tackle all of them at once. Go for low hanging fruit and master the change in that area before moving on. Remember, you didn't get this way overnight so you are not going to change yourself in one week.

3. *Be prepared for haters.* You will have them. The desire to remain the same is strong in HR so prepare yourself to feel ostracized. My advice is to refocus your need for affirmation from your HR colleagues to your client. You will find that your client's affirmation will win you more praise in the long run. Screw trying to appease the HR demigods.

4. *Continuously develop your skills.* Never allow yourself to reside in a place of complacency. Expose

yourself to new challenges and endeavors to further refine your skills as a NakedHR partner. This could include trying new industries or simply learning more about the businesses you support. Whatever your route is, always be on the hustle.

That's all I have. I hope you've learned something by reading this book and more importantly, I hope you share it with your colleagues. My goal is to help transform HR organizations throughout the country and world to be what our employees and clients need us to be: Naked and Unafraid.

References

Bersin, Josh. "Why Simplicity Is The Next Big Thing In HR And Business." Forbes, Forbes Magazine, 25 June 2014, www.forbes.com/sites/joshbersin/2014/06/13/why-simplicity-is-the-next-big-thing-in-hr-and-leadership/.

"Design Thinking 101." Nielsen Norman Group, 2018, www.nngroup.com/articles/design-thinking.

Dierckx, Herwig, et al. "Human Resources: A People or Process Department." Hr Bartender, 19 Oct. 2013, www.hrbartender.com/2013/training/human-resources-a-people-or-process-department/.

Ely, Robin J. "Rethinking Political Correctness." Harvard Business Review, 21 Aug. 2014, hbr.org/2006/09/rethinking-political-correctness.

Folz, Christina. "The 10 Biggest Mistakes New HR Professionals Make." SHRM, SHRM, 11 Apr. 2018, www.shrm.org/hr-today/news/hr-magazine/0218/pages/the-10-biggest-mistakes-new-hr-professionals-make.aspx.

Ford, Valda Boyd. "The Paralysis of Political Correctness." SHRM, SHRM, 11 Apr. 2018, www.shrm.org/hr-today/news/hr-magazine/pages/1107ford.aspx.

Gleeson, Brent. "4 Reasons Process Is Destroying Your Company's Productivity." Forbes, Forbes Magazine, 4 Dec. 2016, www.forbes.com/sites/brentgleeson/2016/12/02/4-reasons-process-is-destroying-your-companys-productivity/#75db47369a1d.

Gurchiek, Kathy. "Knowing the Numbers a Critical HR Skill." SHRM, SHRM, 11 Apr. 2018, www.shrm.org/hr-today/news/hr-news/pages/knowingthenumbersacriticalhrskill.aspx.

"Human Resources Is Not There to Be Your Friend - It's There to Protect the Company." Precedent HR, 12 Feb. 2018, precedenthr.com/human-resources-not-friend-protect-company/.

Kalra, Aditi Sharma. "An Essential Cog in the HR Machinery." Human Resources Online, 15 Aug. 2018, www.humanresourcesonline.net/features/an-essential-cog-in-the-hr-machinery/.

Maimon, Amit. "4 Ways to Guide Your Employees Toward Empowered Decisions." Entrepreneur, Entrepreneur, 23 Dec. 2016, www.entrepreneur.com/article/286971.

Marr, Bernard. "Why Data Is HR's Most Important Asset." Forbes, Forbes Magazine, 13 Apr. 2018, www.forbes.com/sites/bernardmarr/2018/04/13/why-data-is-hrs-most-important-asset/.

McCord, Patty, and Ram Charan. "How Netflix Reinvented HR." Harvard Business Review, 27 June 2016, hbr.org/2014/01/how-netflix-reinvented-hr.

Morgan, Jacob. "What Does The Future Of Human Resources Look Like?" Inc.com, Inc., 21 Nov. 2017, www.inc.com/jacob-morgan/what-does-future-of-human-resources-look-like.html.

Muse, The. "Be The Best Consultant Ever: 6 Things That Will Make You Great." Forbes, Forbes Magazine, 27 Feb. 2017, www.forbes.com/sites/dailymuse/2013/11/05/be-the-best-consultant-ever-6-things-that-will-make-you-great/#629525a495d6.

Muse, The. "Be The Best Consultant Ever: 6 Things That Will Make You Great." Forbes, Forbes Magazine, 27 Feb. 2017, www.forbes.com/sites/dailymuse/2013/11/05/be-the-best-consultant-ever-6-things-that-will-make-you-great/.

O'Donnell, J.T. "HR Is Not Your Friend. Here's Why." Inc.com, Inc., 7 Dec. 2017, www.inc.com/jt-odonnell/what-20-somethings-need-to-know-about-complaining-to-hr.html.

Parmar, Belinda, et al. "People or Process: Which Does Your Company Put First?" World Economic Forum, 2017, www.weforum.org/agenda/2016/09/empathy-index-human-resources-business/.

Ryan, Liz. "Ten Reasons Everybody Hates HR." Forbes, Forbes Magazine, 28 July 2016, www.forbes.com/sites/lizryan/2016/07/27/ten-reasons-everybody-hates-hr/.

University of Basel. "The Brain's Social Network: Nerve Cells Interact like Friends on Facebook." PsyPost, PsyPost, 4 Feb. 2015, www.psypost.org/2015/02/brains-social-network-nerve-cells-interact-like-friends-facebook-31451.